King David

PURSUIT OF THE HEART OF GOD

MIKE HILSON

wesleyan
PUBLISHING HOUSE
wphstore.com
Indianapolis, Indiana

Copyright © 2019 by Mike Hilson
Published by Wesleyan Publishing House
Indianapolis, Indiana 46250
Printed in the United States of America
ISBN: 978-1-63257-324-7
ISBN (e-book): 978-1-63257-325-4
This book was previously self-published as *Coffee with the Pastor,
The Chase: King David's Pursuit of the Heart of God.*

Names: Hilson, Mike, author.
Title: King David : pursuit of the heart of God / Mike Hilson.
Description: Indianapolis : Wesleyan Publishing House, 2019.
| Series: Coffee with the pastor |
Identifiers: LCCN 2018043119 (print) | LCCN 2018054691 (ebook)
| ISBN 9781632573254 | ISBN 9781632573247
Subjects: LCSH: David, King of Israel--Meditations.
Classification: LCC BS580.D3 (ebook) | LCC BS580.D3 H53 2019
(print) | DDC 222/.4092--dc23
LC record available at https://lccn.loc.gov/2018043119

Contents

Acknowledgments

Thank you to my wife, Tina, who has been my partner in life and in ministry. I love you.

To our three boys, Robert, Stephen, and Joshua, thank you for taking this journey of ministry with us and having a great attitude about it along the way. Thank you for growing up to be reliable, solid men on whom I can count, and in whom I take great, godly, pride.

Thank you to my family at New Life Wesleyan Church for giving me the freedom to grow as a leader and as a follower of Christ.

Most importantly, I want to thank and praise God.

About This Book

People sometimes ask why I would take the time to write a book. The answer is twofold. First, it's an opportunity to speak with my children, grandchildren, and great-grandchildren about this wonderful gospel that I have had the honor of working for all of my life. I want them to see the joy and power of living a life guided and protected by God's Word, God's Spirit, and God's commands. In doing so, I hope to establish many generations of my family in the wonderful grace of our Lord. So I write as a father.

I also write as a pastor. New Life Wesleyan Church has become a rather large body of believers meeting in multiple services and multiple locations across multiple states. While this is a huge reason to praise God and more of a blessing than any of us who work here could ever have hoped for, it creates its own set of challenges. It has become impossible for me to sit down individually with folks in the church like I once did and have deeper conversations about the power of God's Word and how it can be applied in their lives. And so, this is the reason for a series of books called *Coffee with the Pastor*.

While I am neither a theologian nor a scholar, as a pastor, it is my job to help people read and better understand the Word of God. His Word is powerful and life changing. If you read and understand it, you can see the God of heaven through the blood of Jesus and the power of the Holy Spirit—and that will change your life. Therefore, the goal of this series of books is not theological, but a practical application of life-changing, biblical truth. That is the purpose of my ministry and the ultimate goal of my life.

So, grab a cup of coffee, open up your Bible, and let us think about what God can do in your life.

Introduction

The life of King David is a wonderful example of the attempt to follow God. While King David was clearly a man after God's heart, he was, by no means, perfect. His flaws and struggles help us understand that a pursuit of the very heart of God is realistic, even for the weakest among us. God does not seek absolute perfection, but a heart that is sold out and focused on him. This is the heart of King David.

King David's story is found in the Bible in 1 Samuel 16 through 1 Kings 2, and also in 1 Chronicles 11—29. This book will focus almost entirely on the account in 1 and 2 Samuel. I encourage you to read the biblical account before you read this book. As you do, keep in mind that you are reading a short biography of one of history's most effective leaders. The lessons here are real and relevant to our daily life decisions and situations.

Rather than track the life of David in chronological order, this book will explore powerful truths from his life and his experience with God. It will do so from six different vantage points of a heart that is sold out to God.

We will consider what we can learn from David's life about developing a godly, courageous, grace-filled, faithful, worshiping heart. Along the way, we will look into what we must do with our flawed heart. Each part will draw from various parts of the life of David, helping us to better understand what God desires from us and how we can properly follow him and his ways.

David was a real guy. He was struggling, winning, bumbling, brilliant, messing up, and doing great things, seemingly all at the same time. Sometimes he had it all together, and other times, he watched it all slip away. King David's most enduring and redeeming quality was not his wisdom (though he had much wisdom), his strength (though he was a strong leader), or his wealth (though he was a wealthy man). His most enduring and redeeming quality was a heart that seemed to ache for the presence and approval of God. We should each strive for such a heart.

As you read your way through this character study, let me point out that this will not cover the entire story of David's life. I will not move through his life verse by verse. Honestly, I see the Old Testament almost entirely as a narrative or a story, while I view much of the New Testament, especially the Epistles, as informative or theological. True, we capture a lot of theology in the stories of the Old Testament, and we capture a lot of narrative in the informative Epistles. This book on David, however, will focus on the narrative of his life. We will move from story to story in the life of this magnificent leader.

So, it's time to get started.

PART 1

A GODLY HEART

The highest calling of mankind is to know and love God. The apostle John describes the importance of knowing and understanding God's love when he says:

Whoever does not love does not know God, because God is love. This is how God showed his love among us: He sent his one and only Son into the world that we might live through him. This is love: not that we loved God, but that he loved us and sent his Son as an atoning sacrifice for our sins. Dear friends, since God so loved us, we also ought to love one another. . . . We love because he first loved us.

—1 John 4:8–11, 19

Proper love is learned and understood in the art of knowing God. Therefore, the most important pursuit in our lives is the pursuit of God. We cannot learn to love our family, spouse, children, or ourselves if we don't first learn the love of God. Understanding and knowing him is what will allow us to truly love, understand, and know those around us as well as ourselves.

This pursuit begins in the heart, so it is our heart that must turn first. People often attempt to change their lives by changing their actions, but the actions of our hands will never alter the attitude of our hearts. Our hearts must be changed, then our actions will follow.

Some may think this talk of love sounds soft and frilly, uncomfortable and weak. But this kind of love is not weak. It is the very basis of strength and courage. This kind of love and godliness gives us hearts that are strong, brave, and brilliantly different. It is what the world around us is looking for, what the God who loves us wants for us.

We'll begin by looking at the heart of King David. Where did he find such a clear understanding of God's heart? How did he remain steady in the face of tremendous challenges? What is it about the heart of David that made him such a great man? What can we learn from David that will help us develop a godly heart?

A Heart for God

"You [King Saul] have done a foolish thing," Samuel said. "You have not kept the command the Lord your God gave you; if you had, he would have established your kingdom over Israel for all time. But now your kingdom will not endure; the Lord has sought out a man after his own heart and appointed him ruler of his people, because you have not kept the Lord's command."

—1 Samuel 13:13–14

What is the most important thing in life? Many would say family or friends, reputation or career, wealth or fame, position or power. Too often, the things we consider important are temporary, having no eternal value. However, if there is any possibility that God exists and cares how I live and feel about him, then I would suggest there is nothing more important than our pursuit of him. We should chase the heart of God, and no one gives us a clearer picture of how to do this than King David.

David became king of Israel after Saul, Israel's first king, died. Saul had started well. He had done a fine job trying to follow God's will and commands, but at some point, things changed. His overall focus shifted from God's priorities to Saul's priorities. This change was Saul's ultimate undoing. Over time, he became jealous and paranoid. He sensed that the presence and blessing of God had left him, and so he became more worried about keeping his job than pleasing his God. He became obsessed to the point of rage and delusions. He pushed away the very people who could have helped him retain the throne—and his sanity. Saul lost sight of God, and in the process, lost everything.

While Saul's heart was turning away from God, a plan for his replacement was taking shape. Far out in the countryside, unknown and unnoticed, was a shepherd boy named David, the youngest son of Jesse. David often sat alone and sang praises to God. During these times of solitude, David's heart, unlike Saul's, was given entirely to the God he would spend his life serving. The questions of importance and commitment were answered long before the challenges and temptations of life were presented. David would not live a perfect life, but he would pursue a perfect love for his God. While Saul's heart was turning away from God, David's heart was turning toward God.

To be honest, God has plenty of Sauls. He has more than enough people who have started out well, only to lose sight of their ultimate calling. God is looking for more Davids. God is seeking men and women who will give their hearts over to him. More than anything else, God desires our hearts to be his. Moses taught us this when he said, "Love the LORD your God with all your heart and with all your soul and with all your strength" (Deut. 6:5). This single phrase became the defining sentence of Jewish religious thought. Its simple power sets all of life in order, if only we heed it. Jesus repeats this command with added emphasis when he says:

"Love the Lord your God with all your heart and with all your soul and with all your mind." This is the first and greatest commandment. And the second is like it: "Love your neighbor as yourself." All the Law and the Prophets hang on these two commandments.

—Matthew 22:37–40

All the law and prophets hang on the command to love God supremely and thereby love others more than we love ourselves.

God is looking for people with hearts sold out to him.

While our list of "important" things may be filled with things that actually are important, there is nothing more important than our relationship with God. Our hearts should be sold out to reaching and pleasing God. In chasing the heart of God, we find the very heart of our purpose in this life. The heart of God will lift us up, just as it took David on an incredible journey from lowly shepherd to godly leader. Are you ready for the trip?

A Heart for Leading

The LORD said to Samuel, "How long will you mourn for Saul, since I have rejected him as king over Israel? Fill your horn with oil and be on your way; I am sending you to Jesse of Bethlehem. I have chosen one of his sons to be king. . . . Jesse had seven of his sons pass before Samuel, but Samuel said to him, "The LORD has not chosen these." So he asked Jesse, "Are these all the sons you have?" "There is still the youngest," Jesse answered. "He is tending the sheep." Samuel said, "Send for him; we will not sit down until he arrives." So he sent for him and had him brought in. He was glowing with health and had a fine appearance and handsome features. Then the LORD said, "Rise and anoint him; this is the one." So Samuel took the horn of oil and anointed him in the presence of his brothers, and from that day on the Spirit of the LORD came powerfully upon David. Samuel then went to Ramah."
—1 Samuel 16:1, 10–13

That day began like any other day in David's life. He was sitting alone watching sheep. It was an unimportant job for an unimportant person. He was truly a nobody. At least he and everyone around him thought he was, but God had other plans. By the end of the day, the prophet Samuel would anoint him king. Anointing a shepherd boy to be the next king? What was Samuel thinking? What was God after?

Keep in mind that David's résumé was not impressive. For the office of king, one would expect the finest schools, great accomplishments, a powerful family, and immense wealth. Kings are born to privilege, not manual labor. Yet God chose this shepherd to be king. God sees what we cannot. God looked into the very soul of this young man and found strength and character fit for a throne. What no one else recognized, God saw as potential. There was more to this young shepherd than met the eye.

Just like David, we may feel alone and forgotten. We may feel like an unimportant person with an unimportant job and an uninteresting life. Truth is, God sees us in a different light. While we tend to the mundane tasks of our daily existence, God shapes us. As David tended his father's sheep, God was shaping him spiritually, physically, and emotionally for the tremendous task that lay ahead of him. In one sense, David's job never changed. He would still watch over someone else's flock, but instead of watching his father's sheep, he would watch over God's chosen people.

While watching sheep, David learned the spiritual art of worship. Many of the Old Testament psalms are songs David wrote to worship God. David might have thought he was just killing time. Bored and alone, he strummed around on his instrument and wrote songs from the emotions that welled up in his heart. He had plenty of time to think and pray. From those thoughts and prayers came the ability to comprehend and communicate the depths of his need for God. This prepared him for the day when he would express the deepest human emotions of praise, elation, sorrow, and despair for an entire nation. David's need for God was not unique to him, and when others heard the cries of his heart, they could relate to his emotion and his desire. From that lonely forgotten place, David found words and music that would inspire an entire nation, and, eventually, an entire world. In that pasture, David had the time to acquire the spiritual insight of a king.

Most of us have lonely times when we feel forgotten and left out. They may be moments when we are asked, or forced, to tend to seemingly unimportant tasks. I call these moments creative boredom, which is a place where God seems to set us aside, for unknown reasons, and forces us to just sit still for a while. As we sit with nothing of apparent value to do, we begin to contemplate, think, pray, and if we get bored enough, maybe even sing. We may believe we are accomplishing nothing, and yet what we create in those hours, days, weeks, months, or even years of isolation, often becomes the base for much of what we will accomplish in the years that follow. God is using those times to develop our thoughts, prayers, faith, and core beliefs. When the day of leadership arrives, along with its pressures, that leadership rests firmly on the well-laid foundation of creative boredom. At that point, God has us right where he has always wanted us.

While David was watching those sheep, he also learned to fight like no one else. David went toe-to-toe with both a lion and a bear. He learned to handle himself in dangerous situations. He learned to pull victory out of what seemed to be impossible situations. He learned to get the upper hand against an opponent who was obviously superior. Having killed wild animals with his bare hands, tall warriors didn't seem so frightening anymore. Nothing seemed impossible for this young shepherd who had already faced death and prevailed. In those fields, David had the opportunity to acquire the powerful, physical ability of a king.

Something else was learned in those lonely days that would be easy to miss. Why did David fight the lion and the bear in the first place? Why was he willing to be there alone in that lousy job? David understood his place as the youngest, his job to protect the sheep, and his duty to his father. Out in the pasture, David came to grips with who he was, and he willingly accepted the assignment he had been given.

Unlike so many talented leaders we know today, David was willing to do the simple and mundane tasks given to him. He did not demand a better job, higher pay, or more respect. He simply accepted who he was and did his job. In that pasture, David learned one of the most profound lessons in all of leadership: great leaders are carved out of great followers.

You cannot achieve greatness as a leader unless you have first learned the art of following. In those lonely fields, David had the opportunity to gain the emotional stability of a king. God was using the mundane to work a miracle. God was preparing the simple to be spectacular. God was preparing the nobody for nobility. A new day was dawning in Israel. No one realized it at the time, and nothing seemed to change. Saul was King, Samuel was the prophet and priest, and David was watching sheep. Although everything seemed normal, there was a new king, and it was a new day.

3

A Heart for Serving

Now the Spirit of the LORD had departed from Saul, and an evil spirit from the LORD tormented him. Saul's attendants said to him, "See, an evil spirit from God is tormenting you. Let our lord command his servants here to search for someone who can play the lyre. He will play when the evil spirit from God comes on you, and you will feel better." So Saul said to his attendants, "Find someone who plays well and bring him to me." One of the servants answered, "I have seen a son of Jesse of Bethlehem who knows how to play the lyre. He is a brave man and a warrior. He speaks well and is a fine-looking man. And the LORD is with him." Then Saul sent messengers to Jesse and said, "Send me your son David, who is with the sheep." So Jesse took a donkey loaded with bread, a skin of wine and a young goat and sent them with his son David to Saul. David came to Saul and entered his service. Saul liked him very much, and David became one of his armor-bearers. Then Saul sent word to Jesse, saying, "Allow David to remain in my service, for I am pleased with him."

—1 Samuel 16:14–22

Now that seems awkward. David, the future king, was in the service of Saul, the current king. David knew that God had rejected King Saul and that it was only a matter of time before he himself sat on the throne that he served. He had already met with Samuel, the prophet, and been anointed to take King Saul's place. Until that time, he needed to be the chief musician and armor-bearer for this rejected king. Really, not a great step-up from the pasture. Better accommodations, tougher audience.

By that time in Saul's life, he was not an easy man to deal with. Holding the position of king, but lacking the presence of the Spirit of God to do the work of a king, Saul had become paranoid, defensive, irrational, and dangerous. He refused to lead Israel into battle against Goliath (see 1 Sam. 17), he hurled spears at David (see 18:10–11), and threatened the life of his own son, Jonathan (see 20:32–33).

Saul was done as king, but he still sat under the crown. All too often leaders outstay their effectiveness. When this happens, the natural outcome is not good. Leaders become leaders, at least in part, because they can read the changing environments around them. They just seem to know when things are changing and are able to change with the times. Therefore, a leader is often able to sense when his or her time is up, but that doesn't mean he or she is willing to let go. That is precisely where King Saul was at this point in his life. And this is never a good situation. When leaders realize they are done, but are not ready or willing to go, they begin to act in defensive and paranoid ways. This causes them to do crazy things that they would otherwise never have even considered.

This is the environment that David walked into. Armed only with his lyre (or harp), he faced an angry, depressed, and, at times, delusional king. David was called to serve this madman. His job was to calm the king's anxiety through music. When it worked, life was great. When it didn't work, he had to dodge flying spears. So how does a person like David work for a clueless king who has almost lost his mind? The answer is found in the heart of a shepherd.

Again, we travel back to that pasture and see the pure brilliance of God's training plan for a king. As a shepherd, David learned great patience. He learned to accept the position he was given in life and work effectively in it. He learned to serve those over whom he really had authority. He learned to serve the very sheep that he ultimately owned. He would shear some of those sheep for their wool, and others he would slaughter for their meat. In the field, he worked as their servant, protector, and guide. In short, David's experience with sheep prepared him for this experience with the king.

All too often, we insist on the best of everything. We want the best job or the best seat, the best paycheck or the best company car. We spend most of our time looking out for number one. The problem is that God has never called us to serve ourselves; he has called us to serve others. God expects us to respect those he has placed in authority over us and to serve them even when they don't seem all that bright or stable, even when we know that one day we will rise above them. God did not call David to a coup attempt. Revolt was not God's plan. God did not lead him to military action or regime change. God simply called him to serve. Quite honestly, that is the greatest training ground for all great leaders. If you cannot serve faithfully, you cannot lead effectively. If you cannot be patient, you cannot be enduringly successful. If you cannot love even madmen, you cannot lead large groups of people. If you cannot remain faithful to where God has placed you today, you will not remain faithful to where God places you tomorrow.

The heart of a king, rightly understood, is the heart of a servant. A true leader will understand and respect the importance of the people he is called to lead.

4

A Heart for Conquering

When David was told, "Look, the Philistines are fighting against Keilah and are looting the threshing floors," he inquired of the LORD, saying, "Shall I go and attack these Philistines?" The LORD answered him, "Go, attack the Philistines and save Keilah." But David's men said to him, "Here in Judah we are afraid. How much more, then, if we go to Keilah against the Philistine forces." Once again David inquired of the LORD, and the LORD answered him, "Go down to Keilah, for I am going to give the Philistines into your hand." So David and his men went to Keilah, fought the Philistines and carried off their livestock. He inflicted heavy losses on the Philistines and saved the people of Keilah.

—1 Samuel 23:1–5

At this point in David's life, he had been anointed king, defeated Goliath, the giant, in battle when no other Israelite soldiers were willing to take him on, and gathered a group of loyal followers, and set out on the run. He was hiding from King Saul who was determined to kill him before he could take the throne. Kind of a rough start to the new job. Likely this life on the run made him miss the boredom of the shepherd's fields. The training regimen for great leaders is rarely a smooth ride, and now we arrive at a new defining moment. In order to become king of Israel, David had to make the transition from being the cool kid who had defeated the great giant in one heroic battle, to being the tested leader who had won many battles and shown the wisdom necessary to lead a nation. Right now, he was just running.

God forced David to begin to change his pattern. David was informed of the plight of Keilah, a town that was just south of where he and his men were staying, and very close to the border of the Philistines, a nation that was a constant enemy of Israel. A band of Philistine raiders would storm into the town, then steal food and valuables from the people of Keilah. This was a common practice in ancient times, and it left the people of Keilah poor and starving. So David asked God what he should do.

God's answer struck fear into the hearts of David's men. Remember, up to this point they had simply been running from King Saul and protecting future King David. They had been playing only defense. Now God wanted them to run an offensive mission against an organized group of fighters. In fact, by defending Keilah, they would be challenging another nation and facing the wrath of yet another king. David's men simply told him "we are afraid" (see 1 Sam. 23:3). So David went back and asked God again. God's answer did not change, but he provided more clarity: "I am going to give the Philistines into your hand" (1 Sam. 23:3–4).

Though David and his men did not realize it, God was beginning to transition David from popular to powerful. This transition is imperative in the life of any leader. Leadership is generally granted to people who are liked. Initial forays into leadership often are based on really shallow qualifications. Looks, strength, talent, and personality all play into these early leadership roles. However, these things alone will never sustain someone in leadership. In the end, there must be production. You must do something in order to be trusted to lead groups, teams, companies, or even nations. Without these moments of testing, there will be no culture of trusting. People will trust you today because of what you accomplished yesterday. So far the only accomplishments David had on his résumé were solitary items. He was good-looking. He knew music. He knew sheep. He knew how to fight bears and lions. He had killed a giant. All of that was cool. However, none of that spoke to his ability to lead. That still had to be proven.

God had just the plan.

This process is similar in our own lives. God gives us talents and abilities from birth. He sends us through lonely times so that we can think through our lives, opinions, and core beliefs. He sends us through challenges so that we can develop our skills at fighting off the "bears" and "lions" and "giants" that will confront us. When the time is right, God sends us opportunities that are at first frightening, but ultimately defining.

David and his men were facing such a moment, and because they accepted the challenge and delivered on the promise of God in their own lives, they became known as David and his "mighty warriors" (see 1 Chron. 11:10).

I don't know what challenges God is allowing in your life right now. I simply know that whatever they are, they are there to refine you and/or define you.

As David sat in those fields watching sheep, convinced, and rightly so, that everyone had forgotten about him, God *refined* him.

As David gave courage to his men and assured them that God was going to give them victory over these Philistines, and through them, deliver the people of Keilah, God *defined* him.

As you go through your own developmental journey, let God refine you. Don't be afraid of the lonely, seemingly unimportant times of creative boredom. Remember that God is using those moments to refine you and develop you into the warrior, the servant, the leader, or the king he always planned for you to be. When God provides challenges (even frightening ones), don't shrink away from them. God will use those moments to define you. Your strength in those moments will always be remembered. Your strength will develop the trust that others will need if they are ever to follow you into even tougher battles and more difficult moments.

5

A Heart for Waiting

Then David went out of the cave and called out to Saul, "My lord the king!" When Saul looked behind him, David bowed down and prostrated himself with his face to the ground. He said to Saul, "Why do you listen when men say, 'David is bent on harming you'? This day you have seen with your own eyes how the LORD delivered you into my hands in the cave. Some urged me to kill you, but I spared you; I said, 'I will not lay my hand on my lord, because he is the LORD's anointed.' See, my father, look at this piece of your robe in my hand! I cut off the corner of your robe but did not kill you. See that there is nothing in my hand to indicate that I am guilty of wrongdoing or rebellion. I have not wronged you, but you are hunting me down to take my life."

—1 Samuel 24:8–11

Patience is a difficult lesson to learn.

Everyone has to learn it.

David, the anointed king of Israel, had an opportunity to move up the ranks quickly. He and his men were running from

King Saul and his army. King Saul had caught up to them, but he didn't yet know it. David and his men, unable to run, hid in a cave. They waited quietly for the angry king to pass by, but as is often the case, things got more complicated. Saul needed to relieve himself, and the cave David and his men were hiding in was where he chose to take care of that business. In other words, the reigning king of Israel walked unknowingly into the hands of the future king of Israel. The scene is actually humorous when you consider it. The king of Israel squatted in front of the man he was seeking to murder—and all of his soldiers—to do his business. Saul was completely unaware and in a completely vulnerable position. King Saul's life was literally in David's hands.

If David had convened a conference call with his advisors to discuss the pros and cons of the situation, the ultimate vote would have no doubt been to kill this crazy king and claim the throne. Note that King Saul had attempted to kill David and even his own son, Jonathan, during senseless fits of rage. Remember that "the Spirit of the Lord had departed from Saul, and an evil spirit from the Lord tormented him" (1 Sam. 16:14). So this king was dealing with the loss of his sanity. Saul was truly crazy—and dangerous. He needed to be silenced. He needed to be replaced. He needed to go. By any reasonable measure, Saul was done. David would have been doing Israel a favor by ending the life, and therefore the reign, of this insane man. You can almost hear the whispers of David's leading men as they crouched behind him in the back of that cave: "Here is your chance, David. Go ahead, kill him." However, David was following more than the guidance of earthly advisors.

In all of this, there is a great lesson: there are no shortcuts to godly maturity.

This same patience is necessary in our own lives. We often want to take charge of the timetable of our advancement. We become willing to bump off someone who is ahead of us in our career or goals, and jump in front of them. When our advancement is the ultimate goal, our integrity will take a hit.

When our *integrity* is the ultimate goal, however, our advancement will take a boost.

David was seemingly ready to take the reins of leadership. He was strong, smart, godly, liked, and successful. David seemed ready for the throne. However, God was not ready to place him there. God still had another man on the throne. The same prophet who anointed David had anointed King Saul. His claim to the throne was every bit as valid as David's claim to the throne—and even more valid because Saul was already there. David needed patience to accept God's timetable.

If David had taken matters into his own hands and violated the anointing that God had placed on Saul as the current reigning King of Israel, he would have proved himself to be no better a king than Saul. He would have set in motion an accepted pattern of murder and bloodshed at the transition of kings. He would have tainted the validity of his own leadership. By waiting and remaining loyal to the insane king who would have killed him, David showed humility, patience, compassion, and strength, and that strength would serve him well in the years to come.

As you consider the virtue of patience, you may question the wisdom of leaving a madman on the throne. Let me bring this into sharper focus. Jesus said, "For in the same way you judge others, you will be judged, and with the measure you use, it will be measured to you" (Matt. 7:2). We simply must be careful, patient, merciful, and kind, even to those who have done or are doing us wrong, because in the end, we are establishing our own outcomes. If David had killed Saul in that cave, he would have spent the rest of his life wondering who was lurking in the back of every cave he entered. Instead, he was able to go to his grave in relative peace. David showed mercy and loyalty, and because of that, he was shown mercy and loyalty all of his days.

We all are given moments that look like opportunities. Moments where we can move ahead a little faster or grab that next promotion or pay raise, and it really wouldn't take much to get it done—just one swipe of a sword, one click of a mouse, one nasty little rumor that, who knows, might be true. If we take that approach, however, we are guilty of trading our integrity for our advancement. Everyone will take notice of the fact that we have done this. They will see us for who we really are, and they will treat us accordingly.

Let's be honest, David could have made a wonderful argument for ridding Israel of this crazy king. He may even have been celebrated for his victory. But his integrity would have suffered a devastating blow. Honestly, there is no throne worth losing your integrity. In fact, the loss of your integrity will ultimately lead to the loss of your security. The loss of your security will ultimately lead to the loss of your peace. The loss of your peace can easily tip over into the loss of sanity and self-worth.

It's true. There are no shortcuts to greatness and godly maturity. But the journey is well worth the effort.

6

A Heart for Self

*Early in the morning Samuel got up and went to meet
Saul, but he was told, "Saul has gone to Carmel. There he
has set up a monument in his own honor and has turned
and gone on down to Gilgal." When Samuel reached
him, Saul said, "The Lord bless you. I have carried out
the Lord's instructions." But Samuel said, "What then is
this bleating of sheep in my ears? What is this lowing of
cattle that I hear?" Saul answered, "The soldiers brought
them from the Amalekites; they spared the best of the
sheep and cattle to sacrifice to the Lord your God, but
we totally destroyed the rest." "Enough." Samuel said to
Saul. "Let me tell you what the Lord said to me last night."
"Tell me," Saul replied. Samuel said, "Although you were
once small in your own eyes, did you not become the
head of the tribes of Israel? The Lord anointed you king
over Israel. And he sent you on a mission, saying, 'Go and
completely destroy those wicked people, the Amalekites;
wage war against them until you have wiped them out.'
Why did you not obey the Lord? Why did you pounce on
the plunder and do evil in the eyes of the Lord?" "But I
did obey the Lord," Saul said, "I went on the mission the
Lord assigned me. I completely destroyed the Amalekites*

and brought back Agag their king. The soldiers took sheep and cattle from the plunder, the best of what was devoted to God, in order to sacrifice them to the Lord your God at Gilgal." But Samuel replied: "Does the Lord delight in burnt offerings and sacrifices as much as in obeying the Lord? To obey is better than sacrifice, and to heed is better than the fat of rams. For rebellion is like the sin of divination, and arrogance like the evil of idolatry. Because you have rejected the word of the Lord, he has rejected you as king."

—1 Samuel 15:12–23

There is a steep cost when leaders fail to follow God.

The story of King Saul is now coming to a close. This man was chosen by God to be the first king over all of Israel. In the early days, he served nobly. His reign was marked with humility and victory. He was a good king, but at some point he lost sight of what really mattered. Saul had fallen into such greed and arrogance that he knowingly violated a direct command of God. He was to completely destroy the Amalekites. Instead of killing their king, he took King Agag as a prisoner, likely as a trophy. Instead of destroying the flocks of the Amalekites, he took the best of those flocks. Now don't get caught up in his insistence that these flocks were for a "sacrifice to the Lord your God." Had King Saul and his men meant to sacrifice these animals, they would have already done so. We have to believe that this greedy and arrogant event is not an isolated one. The pattern of insubordination must have been in place for some time. Here we see the final effect of rebellion against God. God rejected him. "Because you have rejected the word of the LORD, he has rejected you as king" (1 Sam. 15:23).

While the reign of King Saul would last for years to come, the blessing of God's presence in the life of the king had ended. The events of his life spiraled downward from chapters 16 to 31.

Chapter 16: David secretly anointed king.

Chapter 17: David defeats Goliath, a warrior whom Saul should have been facing.

Chapter 18: Saul begins to fear David (vv. 6–9), then begins to lose his mind (vv. 10–11).

Chapter 19: Saul begins to try to kill David.

Chapters 20—27: Saul spends his time and resources pursuing David to kill him.

Chapter 31: Saul attempts to fight without the strength of the Lord, is defeated by the Philistines, and kills himself.

While Saul was allowed by God to retain his throne, they were really tough years both for King Saul and Israel.

When any of us attempt to act in the service of God without the Spirit of God directing us, we just make mistake after mistake. Greatness is not a product of someone being smart, talented, rich, or strong. Greatness is a product of being filled with and surrendered to the indwelling and leadership of the Holy Spirit. Without that power of the Holy Spirit, we lack the ability to make even small decisions effectively. Outwardly we may look the same, but inwardly we lack wisdom, insight, and power. In Saul's final years, he did not cease to be tall, handsome, smart, strong, wealthy, or impressive. He simply began to act without the blessing and guidance of God, and that made all the difference in his leadership and decision-making.

The same truth holds in our lives. When we are surrendered to what the Holy Spirit would have us do, we can perform at levels far beyond our own capacity. When we attempt to operate outside of the guidance of the Holy Spirit, we begin to make decisions that are destructive, divisive, and ultimately, devastating. With just a few moments of self-centered leadership, we can mess up an entire lifetime of Spirit-empowered work.

Overall, Saul had been a good king to this point—until greed overtook him, and God rejected him. That rejection was not a fleeting whim on God's part. It resulted from Saul's repetitive pattern of rejecting God. Saul must have become convinced that he knew how to lead these people better than God did. As soon as that decision was made, his reign was effectively over.

It is better to have the anointing of God while hiding in a cave than to sit on a throne without the powerful, life-changing presence of the Holy Spirit.

7

A Heart for Following

After the king [David] was settled in his palace and the Lord had given him rest from all his enemies around him, he said to Nathan the prophet, "Here I am, living in a house of cedar, while the ark of God remains in a tent." Nathan replied to the king, "Whatever you have in mind, go ahead and do it, for the Lord is with you."

—2 Samuel 7:1–3

Finally, King David reigned on the throne of Israel. He had conquered the entire nation of Israel and expanded her borders. He had defeated any internal challenges to the throne and had shown the capacity to defeat any external enemies that would even consider attacking his nation. He had finally come to a place of relative peace. At such a moment, many people would choose to sit back and do a little "profit taking." They would enjoy the spoils of their labor and live it up for a while. Honestly, who can blame them? David had worked hard and risked much to get to this place. It is astonishing that he had even survived the process. No one would begrudge him taking some time to just be blessed.

That was not how the mind of this king worked.

Instead of just enjoying the spoils of all his victories, King David yearned to do something to bring glory to God. The Lord had placed David on the throne, and David knew it. He spent his entire life keenly aware that it was only the blessing of God that sustained him and gave him victory and wisdom. So he made a decision to build a great temple to honor God and to place the ark of God within the temple. The prophet Nathan must have thought it a great idea, since he said, "Whatever you have in mind, go ahead and do it, for the Lord is with you" (2 Sam. 7:3). Nathan was probably thinking that God blessed everything David did, so why not go for it?

But wait. Stop. God *never* blesses everything *anybody* does. No one has that kind of pass with God.

Not even King David.

God only blesses what he commands. He will give you the strength, resources, opportunity, and wisdom to accomplish everything he has planned for you to do. When you attempt to start doing what God has planned for someone else, you run against the will of God and could suddenly find yourself acting in arrogance instead of humility. God humbles the proud but lifts up the humble. King David and the prophet Nathan were about to get a wake-up call.

"The LORD declares to you that the LORD himself will establish a house for you: When your days are over and you rest with your ancestors, I will raise up your offspring to succeed you, your own flesh and blood, and I will establish his kingdom. He is the one who will build a house for my Name, and I will establish the throne of his kingdom forever."

—2 Samuel 7:11–13

Later that night, while Nathan was asleep, God spoke to him in a vision and basically said (in my own words): "You guys got that all wrong. Stop assuming that since I have blessed David in the past that I will just choose to bless anything he does. Talk to me before you declare my blessing." My guess is that prophet Nathan could not get to King David fast enough the next morning. I imagine it going something like this: He jumped out of bed running toward the palace yelling, "King. We got it all wrong. You can't build a temple . . . but your son will."

Now, the first lesson we need to learn is a phrase that I have used repeatedly over the years as I have worked to plan and lead. Listen to these words carefully and I would suggest you commit them to memory:

There is a fine line between faith and presumption.

Faith moves with the confidence of God's blessing—and does great things. Presumption moves into places God has not blessed or preordained and assumes that God will bless it anyway—which tends to make a mess. King David and the prophet Nathan had just moved from faith in the God who had always provided, into presuming to know what God wanted without asking him, and they almost made a huge mess.

The second lesson to be learned here comes from King David's response.

"Who am I, Sovereign Lord, and what is my family, that you have brought me this far? And as if this were not enough in your sight, Sovereign Lord, you have also spoken about the future of the house of your servant."

—2 Samuel 7:18–19

King David immediately bowed before God.

This, I believe, was the defining characteristic of King David. He had the capacity to lead in the face of insurmountable odds, the strength to endure unbelievable hardship, and the wisdom to decide great and weighty matters, and yet, he *never* forgot that he was the servant of God. He never stopped being the humble, obedient shepherd. If it was God's will that someone else build the temple, then so be it.

Praise God for what he allows us to do instead of whining about what he does not allow us to do. We need to learn this lesson. We would be happier people. We would be more content. Ultimately, we would be more effective. Our constant striving toward what God has given to others causes anger and resentment in our hearts and minds. We even begin to blame God for not giving us everything we want, but God never promised to give us everything we want. He only promised to provide for all of our needs. Our happiness and contentment, our peace and security, are not based on the fact that we kept up with whoever is the latest and greatest. Our peace and security are based on the fact that we are serving the almighty God of heaven. He is the one who has chosen our place in this world. He made that choice because it is the best choice for us. He made that choice because we will excel in it, and because we will find peace and fulfillment in it. When we spend time whining because we weren't given someone else's blessing, we fail to give God the glory for the blessing he has given us.

PART 2

A COURAGEOUS HEART

If we're to make a difference in the world around us, in addition to having godly hearts, we'll also need courageous hearts. That's because we are bound to face terrifying moments along the way. Giant problems will come at us with menacing faces and insurmountable weapons. There will likely be horrible days and difficult, lengthy battles to fight in order to achieve and maintain our freedom from sin and the bondage it brings. We must be people of courage, or we will simply cower in a corner and never prevail. But there will also be friends who stand by us in those battles. There will be people who share their confidence and faith with us when we lack our own confidence and faith.

As I said earlier, a godly heart is anything but weak and defenseless. Godly patience is different from fearful avoidance. Don't confuse godliness with weakness. Instead, understand and remember that the heart surrendered to God is a heart filled with courage and power.

8

One Giant Problem!
The Right Perspective

David said to Saul, "Let no one lose heart on account of this Philistine; your servant will go and fight him."
—1 Samuel 17:32

When our children were younger, my wife, Tina, and I would take regular summer trips to theme parks. Generally, Tina would spend time with whichever one of our boys wasn't comfortable or not yet tall enough for the roller coasters while I took the others for the ride. I have always enjoyed roller coasters. One particular day, we were toward the end of our time at the park when the boys asked me to ride an indoor coaster with them. I agreed, because it was actually a great ride. This coaster was enclosed in a large structure, and the darkness and lighting effects gave the illusion that you were in a space battle. Like I said, it was a great ride. Well, as we came to the end of the ride, having passed through a couple of loops and hills and turns, the coaster was supposed to suddenly turn itself right side up directly out of a corkscrew and then emerge into the light.

I had ridden this coaster many times before with no trouble. However, when we came out of that final corkscrew and leveled back out into the light, something happened in my head. I looked forward, and the train station that was at the end of the ride was completely sideways. I knew this could not actually be true, but it is exactly what my mind was seeing. Then bam. My reality shifted back to normal. The shift was so sudden and shocking that it made me dizzy. I was a bit nauseous and shaken. When the ride was over, I carefully walked my way out of the station toward my wife who was waiting outside. I was struggling to not show any signs of my problem to the boys, but I felt really weird. I sat down and whispered to my wife how I was feeling. I began to wonder how such a thing could happen. That train station was never sideways. What my mind saw at the end of that tunnel was never true, and yet it is exactly what I saw. It was all I could see. Hard as I tried, I could not see that moment any other way.

The army of Israel had a similar experience. They saw something in a very skewed way, and it caused fear, nausea, and immobility. The Philistine army was challenging the army of Israel, but the Philistines had decided that this battle would be different. They marched out their champion. Goliath was over nine feet tall and wielded weapons that almost no one in Israel's army could even lift. The challenge was simple. The Philistines would send out Goliath and the Israelites would send out their champion. If Goliath killed their champion, then Israel would serve the Philistines. If Israel's champion killed

Goliath, then the Philistines would serve Israel. That is a lot of pressure on one man to be "champion."

No one from Israel's army stepped forward.

Not even King Saul.

Now Saul had been described this way when Samuel first found him and anointed him king: "Saul, as handsome a young man as could be found anywhere in Israel, and he was a head taller than anyone else" (1 Sam. 9:2). Yes, King Saul was the tallest guy around—big and strong, tall and well trained. If anyone were to take on Goliath, it should have been King Saul, but he sat in his tent and did nothing. He was just as afraid of failure as the rest of the army.

That is one of the dangers of a skewed perspective. It is highly contagious. From the moment Goliath stepped out on the battlefield and challenged the army of Israel, everyone knew that King Saul should be the one to fight him. But he didn't. He was afraid, and his fear spread like wildfire in the camp until no one was willing to fight. No one would take the risk—until David arrived.

The same spirit of fear that had overtaken the rest of the army did not seem to affect David. From his perspective, he saw no giant. He saw no formidable foe. He saw no threat. He only saw an "uncircumcised Philistine" who was arrogant enough to "defy the armies of the living God" (1 Sam. 17:26). David's perspective was not frozen on the size of the challenge or the penalty of failure; his focus was placed firmly on the honor of the God of Israel. David was not offended that Goliath had insulted Israel's army; he was infuriated that Goliath had insulted Israel's God. Since David's focus was on God, he could clearly see that Goliath was the one in trouble. Unlike all the others, David looked at Goliath and saw nothing more than an opportunity for God to show himself faithful.

In our lives, we must be careful with our perspective. There will undoubtedly come days when our perspective is skewed. Those days can cause dizziness, nausea, disorientation, and fear. The belief that we must slay giants on our own and be the champion for everyone else while the whole world watches is terrifying. If we can just keep our focus on God, then we will remember that those terrifying moments will pass. Soon enough, our vision will correct itself, and God will deliver us from whatever giant we may be facing at the moment. Then we will realize that we never really had to be the champion at all. We just needed to trust God. He is always bigger than any giant who comes our way. He is always providing all that we need. Even when the odds seem insurmountable, he is always more than enough to overcome all odds.

We don't need to be everyone's champion; we just need to keep our eyes on God who is champion for all.

9

One Giant Problem!
The Right Practice

Saul replied, "You are not able to go out against this Philistine and fight him; you are only a young man, and he has been a warrior from his youth." But David said to Saul, "Your servant has been keeping his father's sheep. When a lion or a bear came and carried off a sheep from the flock, I went after it, struck it and rescued the sheep from its mouth. When it turned on me, I seized it by its hair, struck it and killed it. Your servant has killed both the lion and the bear; this uncircumcised Philistine will be like one of them, because he has defied the armies of the living God. The LORD who rescued me from the paw of the lion and the paw of the bear will rescue me from the hand of this Philistine."

—1 Samuel 17:33–37

Don't get the idea that David simply strolled out onto the battlefield to face Goliath with no prior fighting experience. No, he was not a soldier. He had not received any formal training in warfare. But he did have experience. David had courage to fight that day because he had been practicing courage for years.

Now, I find it humorous to imagine how King Saul must have felt as he listened to David talk. Here's my version. The king looks at this boy and comes to the only logical conclusion: "You can't fight this giant. You're just a kid." Then David responds, "No, I have been watching my father's sheep."

Pause.

What must be going through King Saul's mind right here? I imagine him saying: "Watching sheep? That qualifies you to fight a giant? Kid, you are making my point, not yours."

King Saul must have been somewhere between horrified and amused at the thought of this child going out to fight a giant.

Then David must have said (again, here's my version): "Look, I have already killed lions and bears without any big, nasty weapons. God kept me alive through that, so I am absolutely confident that he will be with me now. If God can keep me safe and give me victory over a lion and a bear, this oversized punk is no problem."

I imagine the king replied: "OK, go for it."

I doubt that King Saul had any real faith that David would prevail that day. Maybe he was making plans for some counteroffensive, using the fight between David and Goliath as a distraction. It's hard to believe that the king of Israel actually placed the future of his nation into the hands of a boy, with no backup plan. Then again, Saul failed to remember the great weapon that David would carry onto that battlefield. Faith.

Not just any faith—a practiced faith. David was not afraid, because he had faced this kind of fear before. The real fear had come the first time he faced a lion or a bear. It was then that he wondered if he would survive. As God delivered David time and again, the fear began to subside, and it was replaced with humble, thankful courage that placed its confidence in God's hands, not his own. That confidence would now enter battle with him. If God could empower him to kill a lion, how hard could a giant be? The logic is simple and yet profound. That kind of faith only comes through practice.

When I was in high school, I was a choir kid. Our teacher taught us the different parts of a song by making us sing them over and over until we were sick of hearing them. As she did this, she often said, "I want these notes so burned into your brain that if I came to your house at two o'clock in the morning and woke you up, you would sing them perfectly from memory." Now, I knew she was never going to show up at my house at two o'clock, but she was going to make those notes so familiar that there would be no fear left in singing them no matter how large the crowd or how tough the competition. Faith works the same way. The more you use it, the stronger it grows. Over time, you build up a reservoir of deliverance stories (lions and bears) that make other challenges (giants) seem quite manageable.

So, if you are ever going to face the "giants" in your life, you must start by killing "lions."

If you are ever going to kill the "lions" in your life, you must start by killing "bears."

If you are ever going to kill the "bears" in your life (I am making an assumption here about David's life), you must start by killing "wolves."

If you are ever going to kill the "wolves" in your life, you must start by killing "foxes."

If you are ever going to kill the "foxes" in your life, you must start by watching "sheep."

If you are ever going to watch "sheep" in your life, you must start by humbly accepting the work you have been given.

Then, by caring about the sheep and depending on God, you become the ultimate giant slayer.

It just takes practice.

10

One Giant Problem!
The Right Approach

David said to the Philistine, "You come against me with sword and spear and javelin, but I come against you in the name of the LORD Almighty, the God of the armies of Israel, whom you have defied.

—1 Samuel 17:45

OK, King Saul must have been thinking that if David was going to die, the least he could do was make sure that David was well-equipped. The king put his armor on the shepherd, and it didn't fit. After all, King Saul was a full head taller than anyone else in Israel, and David was just a boy. So you can imagine what Saul's armor must have looked like on David. Refusing the armor, since it would only get in his way, David took up his staff, his sling, and five smooth stones, carefully chosen from a nearby stream.

Off he went to fight Goliath.

Again, pause and consider what King Saul and all those around him must have been thinking: "This kid is crazy. What have we done? He is gonna get killed. This won't last long."

Then, as David entered the field of battle, all of the soldiers got their first look at the champion of Israel. Their hearts must have fallen to their feet. It must have been terrifying, insulting, and devastating all at the same time. Terrifying, because there was no logical way this kid would kill that giant. Insulting, because every single one of those soldiers was better prepared and more suitable for this task than David. Devastating, because each one was forced to face the ugly truth that none of them—not one—had the courage to volunteer. But this kid had, and there he went with no armor, no sword, no spear, and no helmet. Just a stick, a sling, and some rocks.

It wasn't looking good.

David understood something that all of us need to learn. God has gifted each of us differently. The tools each of us need for a battle or challenge may differ. King Saul had graciously offered David his own armor for battle. He was sincerely trying to equip this kid for what was ahead of him. But that wasn't what David needed. In fact, if David had gone out to fight Saul's way, he likely would have lost. He didn't need to fight like a warrior, but like a shepherd.

When Tina and I first entered ministry, plenty of people told us exactly what we had to do to be successful. The list was daunting. Wear a suit. Carry a KJV (King James Version) Bible. Pray five hours every day. Study five hours every day. Visit everyone in the church at least once a month. Visit the elderly at least once a week. Provide counseling services to everyone in the congregation. Keep your office clean. Always be in the office between the hours of 8 a.m. and 5 p.m. Keep the church building clean. Teach Sunday school. Lead the choir. Preach like some combination of Billy Graham and John Wesley. Keep everyone happy so no one leaves. Bring in new people. And the list continued far longer than I have time or space for here.

It was impossible.

I remember having to come to grips with the fact that I could not do all of that. In fact, I didn't even want to do most of it. So Tina and I simply decided that we could not fight the battle in someone else's armor. We were going to have to pastor like us and not like anyone else. Yes, there were those who told us that we were doing it all wrong, and they still do. There were those who told us we were going to fail, and they still do. We knew that we could not face this giant called ministry in armor that didn't fit us.

Your life is no different. No matter what your career or your challenges, there will always be well-meaning people who insist you do things exactly the way they do. They insist that if you are going to succeed, you must follow a particular plan in very specific ways. There are some careers and activities that require strict adherence to a given pattern. When baking anything, you must follow the instructions exactly to get a proper outcome.

However, much of life *isn't* like that. Much of life is really a matter of finding out what mix of gifts, talents, and abilities God has given you, and then learning to navigate the challenges, using the tools you already have. Following someone else's pattern may or may not help.

This is why diets and workout regimens can be such fads. The diet that works for one person just doesn't work for another. The exercise plan that works for one just doesn't work for all. A friend of mine who is a trainer once said something profound to me: "The best workout plan you can have is the one *you* will follow." Likewise, the best plan of action for whatever battles you may face is the plan of action that fits who *you* are and how *you* function.

Finding this balance requires a clear understanding of several things. First, you need faith in a God who has equipped and prepared you to face the challenges that are in front of you. This faith will keep you from becoming discouraged or overwhelmed. Second, you need to be in the practice of spending time with God through his Word, prayer, worship, church services, and more, so that you can learn to hear his voice and understand his will for your life. This perspective and practice will ultimately guide you in finding the right armor for the battle ahead. If you are a shepherd, then by all means fight like a shepherd. If you are a warrior, then by all means fight like a warrior. God has prepared you for the battles that lay ahead of you, and he expects you to fight like you, not like anyone else.

So get your stick, find some smooth stones, pick up your sling, and let go.

One Important Friend

*Jonathan said to David, "Go in peace, for we have sworn
friendship with each other in the name of the Lord, saying,
'The Lord is witness between you and me, and between
your descendants and my descendants forever.'" Then
David left, and Jonathan went back to the town.*
—1 Samuel 20:42

When David first arrived at the king's residence to play the
harp for King Saul, he struck up a friendship with the king's son,
Jonathan. These two became best friends who fully trusted and
supported one another. Together, they faced many trials, and
likely many triumphs, in their younger years. Jonathan could
always count on David, and David could always count on
Jonathan.

This friendship became strained and awkward once King
Saul started to lose his mind. When Saul began to fear David
and set his mind to kill him, Jonathan wouldn't have any part
in it. Saul argued with Jonathan saying:

*"You son of a perverse and rebellious woman! Don't I
know that you have sided with the son of Jesse to your
own shame and to the shame of the mother who bore
you? As long as the son of Jesse lives on this earth,
neither you nor your kingdom will be established. Now
send someone to bring him to me, for he must die!"*

—1 Samuel 20:30–31

When Jonathan refused to turn over David, King Saul hurled
a spear in an attempt to kill his own son. Saul's motives began
at protecting the family and ended in madness.

Jonathan knew that his father was right. He knew that he
would never be king and that David would follow his father
on the throne. Later, in a brief conversation, Jonathan told
David: "Don't be afraid. . . . My father Saul will not lay a hand
on you. You will be king over Israel, and I will be second to
you. Even my father Saul knows this" (1 Sam. 23:17). Both
Jonathan and Saul knew that their family's reign over Israel
would not continue, but their reaction to that knowledge could
not have been more different.

The friendship between David and Jonathan was the stuff
of legend. Jonathan loved and trusted David so much that he
was willing to serve in David's kingdom rather than be king
of his own kingdom. David trusted Jonathan so much that he

followed Jonathan's lead in matters concerning Jonathan's father, Saul. David would have rather been killed by Saul than bring sorrow to Jonathan. In the end, Jonathan did not survive to serve in David's kingdom. King Saul entered an ill-advised battle against the Philistines, and Jonathan was killed in battle. (We will talk more about this later.) Jonathan and David remained true to one another and true to the friendship that would span into the next generation.

Every one of us needs a friend like that—one who will stand by us against all odds, one we can trust implicitly, one we can tell everything to. This kind of friendship gives strength in tough times, courage in frightening times, comfort in painful times, and joy in happy times. This kind of friendship makes life brighter, better, deeper. Friendship like this gives life more meaning. The grand question is how do you find a friend like that?

The answer is really rather simple and yet very difficult to accomplish. Here are three thoughts.

Be friendly.

The passage doesn't specifically mention this, but when Jonathan and David first met, I imagine David was friendly to the young heir to the throne. He was probably also a little bit intimidated and somewhat afraid. Here before David, the one anointed to be the next king of Israel, was the guy who was actually first in line to the throne. Soon, however, they were just two boys who got along and liked each other's company. This is a painfully simple lesson that many could stand to learn. If you are not friendly, you will not have friends. Seems obvious, doesn't it? Yet so many people miss it. They go through life grumpy, angry, or bitter, and then they wonder why they don't have friends. They have no friends because no one wants to hang out with them. Who wants to be around a grump, complainer, or whiner? Be friendly so that you can find friends.

Be trustworthy.

Perhaps the greatest part of having a true friend is the fact that you can trust them with anything you need to say. A true friend is going to look out for your best interests and is not going to spew your secrets to the world. True friends can be trusted with anything. Everyone needs someone they trust with the deepest, darkest, most embarrassing parts of who they are. These people are rare. No one has an overabundance of these friends. So we must figure out how to find a trustworthy friend.

The answer is not as complex as you might think. Simply put, if you are not trustworthy, you will have a really difficult time finding friends who can be trusted. Have you ever wondered why certain friends of yours are well balanced and live mostly peaceful lives while others live in constant chaos? Trustworthy people tend to attract trustworthy people; likewise, liars and cheats attract liars and cheats. What if attracting liars and cheats comes naturally to you, but you want to attract trustworthy friends so that you can change? Well, as we talked about earlier, you can't change the actions of your hands without changing the attitude of your heart. Ask the Holy

Spirit to start changing your heart so that you can become the trustworthy friend you are attempting to find. When you are trustworthy and those around you are trustworthy, you can climb out of the chaos and find peace.

Life without people you can trust is a frightening thought. Be trustworthy so that you can find people who can be trusted.

Be loyal.

Jonathan was completely loyal to David. He protected, helped, defended, and trusted him. In the end, Jonathan remained loyal to both his father and to David, which established his own family's place in the kingdom. Even though Jonathan didn't survive to serve alongside David, his loyalty was never forgotten. We talk about it to this day. We honor that kind of commitment to another person. In fact, this is the kind of friendship we all desire.

Throughout my life, God has put people in my path that have become these kinds of friends. They listened as I emotionally collapsed. They understood as I irrationally feared. They forgave as I personally failed. The one thing they have never done is leave; that kind of staying power matters. The greatest example of this in my life is my relationship with my wife, Tina. I can face anything in life as long as I have God and her by my side. I know she will always be here. That's one thing we both decided on when we chose to get married. No matter what, we would be there for each other. That kind of loyalty brings stability, strength, and peace.

Find that kind of loyalty. Be that kind of loyal. When you find a friend who can be trusted, remain loyal to them, and in doing so, you will find them remaining loyal to you.

Summing this up is rather simple.

To have a friend, be a friend.

To find trustworthy friends, be a friend who can be trusted.

To find loyal friends, be loyal to your friends.

That kind of friendship is possible—and legendary.

12

One Horrible Day

Now the Philistines fought against Israel; the Israelites fled before them, and many fell dead on Mount Gilboa. The Philistines were in hot pursuit of Saul and his sons, and they killed his sons Jonathan, Abinadab and Malki-Shua. The fighting grew fierce around Saul, and when the archers overtook him, they wounded him critically. Saul said to his armor-bearer, "Draw your sword and run me through, or these uncircumcised fellows will come and run me through and abuse me." But his armor-bearer was terrified and would not do it; so Saul took his own sword and fell on it. When the armor-bearer saw that Saul was dead, he too fell on his sword and died with him. So Saul and his three sons and his armor-bearer and all his men died together that same day.

—1 Samuel 31:1–6

This was truly a dark day in Israel.

While King Saul had been in failing mental health for some years now, it was still a terrible thing to lose your king, his sons, and his army all in one day. The Philistines had won a great victory, and Saul had lost everything. He had tried for years to kill David in order to ensure his place, and ultimately Jonathan's place, on the throne. In the end, though, he watched three of his sons die and his army be routed. Finally, he realized that the Philistines were coming for him. They would not be satisfied until they had his dead body as a trophy. So in order to deny them the honor of killing the king of Israel, Saul fell on his own sword and died. His armor-bearer, who had remained faithfully by his side throughout this entire fierce battle, then did the same. So the reign of King Saul came to a violent end.

It didn't have to go down that way.

Earlier, we looked at the story of God rejecting Saul because of his arrogance, greed, and lack of obedience. At the end of that discussion, the prophet Samuel declared to King Saul, "I will not go back with you. You have rejected the word of the LORD, and the LORD has rejected you as king over Israel." (1 Sam. 15:26). While that is one instance of Saul's failure, the truth is that the failure to obey God had become a pattern. This incident was simply the final straw. Saul consistently failed to follow God's commands, and the ultimate result was that God rejected him as king over Israel. There are some very important lessons to be learned here.

Sin has consequences.

The reason Saul, his sons, and his army died at the hands of the Philistines on that horrible day can be found in God's rejection of Saul. While God is gracious and forgiveness is always available, sin has consequences. We will always pay the price for sin. There are no exceptions. In fact, the more we try to avoid the consequences, the more likely others will be harmed by our poor choices. God did not reject Jonathan and his brothers. However, since their father, Saul, chose to fight on without the blessing of God, they paid the price for his sin and stubbornness. The armor-bearer was in no way guilty of the sins that Saul had committed, and yet he, too, paid the ultimate price for the king's failure.

In our lives, sin will cost us. If we are not careful, it can cost those who are closest to us as well. Family, closest friends, supporters and coworkers can be harmed by the consequences of our sin. The higher you are on the leadership ladder, the more people you put in danger with your own sin. Never assume that God will overlook your sin. Always remember that there will be consequences for your actions. Always assume that the consequences of your sins will reach across to those you want to protect and hurt them as well. Choose your actions prayerfully and carefully.

Effectiveness is gone when God's blessing is lifted.

From the moment that God rejected Saul as king, his reign was over. He held the job for quite a while longer, but he was done. This is a really tough truth to come to grips with, even for those around us. The prophet Samuel had hoped for God to have a change of heart:

The LORD said to Samuel, "How long will you mourn for Saul, since I have rejected him as king over Israel? Fill your horn with oil and be on your way; I am sending you to Jesse of Bethlehem. I have chosen one of his sons to be king."

—1 Samuel 16:1

God had already moved on, while Samuel and Saul were still holding on. Now Samuel did move on, but not Saul. The remainder of his time on the throne of Israel was marked by bad choices, anger, resentment, delusion, and paranoia. This is what happens when we try to continue to work in God's kingdom without God's blessing. Our effectiveness is entirely wrapped up in his presence, guidance, and blessing. Our effectiveness is *his* work, not ours. When God says he is done with us, the blessing is gone.

When God says you are done, move on.

The final lesson here is really quite simple. When you realize that God is done with you, get out of the way. You may ask: "But who will lead if I leave?" Remember, God has already anointed someone to take your place. Your replacement is simply hiding in a cave somewhere waiting for you to recognize the obvious. Everyone else sees it. Everyone else knows you are done. Everyone else is waiting for you to move on so they can move on.

Now, that does not mean that when God is done with us, we must literally fall on a sword and die. No, it means that God is done with us in that particular endeavor. God is gracious and merciful. If we are willing to move on, he will move with us, as long as we strive to seek him and his kingdom. The consequences of staying when God has told us to go are always high.

I heard a preacher say recently that the cost of concealment is always higher than the cost of confession. What a great truth.

What we need to take from this horrible ending to the life of King Saul is a warning. Stay close to God and strive with all that is in you to follow his leading, even when it doesn't match your preference. What you ultimately need is his blessing. God clearly prefers obedience to sacrifice (see 1 Sam. 15:22).

Follow him closely.

Obey him completely.

Surrender to him fully.

Pray that you can remain so committed and focused that you will never leave his blessing, and therefore have to move out of his way to remain in his will.

13

One Difficult Battle

The war between the house of Saul and the house of David lasted a long time. David grew stronger and stronger, while the house of Saul grew weaker and weaker.
—2 Samuel 3:1

A kingdom, organization, or family left behind by someone who has operated in an atmosphere of paranoia, fear, anger, and/or delusion is extremely difficult to bring back together. These elements, so evident in Saul's final years on the throne, are horribly destructive within any group of people. When the head of the group operates in paranoia, fear, anger, and/or delusion, the entire group becomes organized around these terribly destructive forces. People begin to build protection for themselves rather than building what is best for the group. Leaders under the king begin to pad their own futures without concern for the people they are supposed to be serving. Eventually, the entire leadership, many layers deep, is entrenched and unmovable because they are all paralyzed by fear.

Now David, who had been anointed Israel's king, had to jump into this environment and attempt to bring the nation back together. He had to begin by defeating all of the other claims to leadership within the borders of the nation, but he had to do this in the right way. He couldn't be murderous or vindictive in his actions. He had to somehow allow God's timing to bring about God's ending. Not everyone is so patient. Like any dysfunctional group or person, a deep and painful struggle for ultimate control begins. David, if he was ever to be an effective king, had to navigate that struggle with God's help and direction.

Now, let's look at this situation as if Israel were a single person and not a nation. In fact, let's look at it from the perspective of Israel representing *you*. Within you, there are warring factions that are each looking to take control of the driver's seat of your life. And you, the one to whom God has given responsibility over your kingdom, must choose those whom you will work with, restrain, and destroy. Each of these approaches will be required along the way.

Abner—The Influence of Pride and the Pursuit of Power

Abner, the commander of Saul's army, took matters into his own hands (see 2 Sam. 3:1–39). He realized that David would most likely choose someone else to be head of his army and that this would leave Abner either unimportant or dead. So he immediately set up one of Saul's remaining sons as king. Abner knew that Samuel had anointed David to be king, but he wanted to protect his own position. There are times when it seems easier to go back to the brokenness of your past than to do the work of healing. This is exactly how old habits and temptations act within us. We know that they must go, if God's will is to prevail. Our minds and spirits will know that a given habit, temptation, relationship, or sin is in opposition to God's will and must go, and yet we still defend its existence in our lives. Somewhere deep within us, there is an Abner who is trying to put the sin of our past back on the throne of our lives. We can't let that happen.

So Abner found himself opposing David and therefore opposing God. He set up a neighboring kingdom to Israel and placed a son of Saul on the throne, so that he could maintain some level of his position and power. For two years, the battle between David and Ish-Bosheth, Saul's son and Abner's puppet king, raged on. This seemed to take forever, just like the battles within us against long-held habits, hurts, and hang-ups. Just think about it. You spent years, perhaps decades, establishing that habit within your life. Now, because there is a new king on the throne of your life (Jesus), that long-held and deeply established thing has to go. It's not going to go quietly or easily. It's going to fight for its existence, power, and place. You must defeat it with the power of the Holy Spirit so that you can give full glory to the God who saved you and now controls you. The day of victory will come. David, by the power of God, won the day. Not, however, before Abner, Ish-Bosheth, and many others were dead.

Your hurts, habits, and hang-ups are not to be controlled. They are to be destroyed. It may be that you need to hold some kind of personal, perhaps even private ceremony—a ceremony that only includes you and God—to finally let go. David held an honorable funeral for Abner. He knew Abner had to go. He knew Abner was destructive. He knew Abner was a problem. He also knew that Abner was a very real and important part of the Israel's history, part of Israel's story. Although he had to be removed, he needed to be remembered. And so it is with our hurts, habits, and hang-ups. They are a very real, important part of who we are as individuals. Although they may need to go, they should not be forgotten.

Eventually, David conquered the city of Jerusalem, and God allowed him to give the city its nickname, the city of David. The city clearly belonged to God, but God allowed David to be known as the one who conquered it . . . even to this day. Isn't that wonderful? My life belongs to God, but he is willing to allow me to be known as the one who conquered it.

Ish-Bosheth—The Foolishness of Fame and Materialism

Meanwhile, Abner son of Ner, the commander of Saul's army, had taken Ish-Bosheth son of Saul and brought him over to Mahanaim. He made him king over Gilead, Ashuri and Jezreel, and also over Ephraim, Benjamin and all Israel.

—2 Samuel 2:8–9

Here we find the account of Ish-Bosheth, son of Saul, being set up as king over part of the nation of Israel, but notice something in these verses. Ish-Bosheth was never the one in charge; Abner was. Ish-Bosheth may have worn the crown, but Abner held the power. So, why would Ish-Bosheth allow such an obviously unflattering situation to exist? Because Ish-Bosheth was a foolish man.

Ish-Bosheth was after fame, materialism, and wealth. He wanted the trappings of power without the responsibility of serving as king. He wanted the meal plan, but not the workload. That is precisely what Abner was offering. Ish-Bosheth got to live in a palace, wear fine clothes, shop wherever he wanted, eat the finest food, hang out with the beautiful people, and be the center of attention at all of the best parties.

Life was great.

Except for one little thing: he was a puppet and everyone knew it. When Ish-Bosheth walked into the room, everyone showed respect to him out of fear for Abner. They all knew that Ish-Bosheth held no power. They knew that he was just *acting* like an important man. All the fluffy clothes, sparkly jewelry, big parties, and grandiose proclamations were just for show. In reality, he was a fraud. He looked completely foolish.

Our pursuit of fame and wealth often has a similar effect on us. Neither fame nor wealth in and of itself is a bad thing. Both can be given by God and used powerfully for his kingdom. However, when fame or wealth becomes our god, we begin to look foolish, and everyone else can see it. Life is about so much more than what we own or how we are known. Life is about who we belong to and what we have done. When we spend our lives focused inwardly, we begin to ignore what we look like outwardly. Now I know that seems backwards. Self-centered people are always worried about what they look like to others.

Actually, not really.

They are worried about what they think they look like in front of others. They are so blinded by their own materialism and popularity that they never even realize that everyone else sees right through the facade. Everyone knows that beauty has no depth. Everyone knew that Ish-Bosheth had no power, and yet he was clueless. It's no mistake that the name Ish-Bosheth means "man of shame." While he could have used his position as a son of Saul to bring peace, he used his desire for fame and fortune to bring war and destruction. In the process, he proved himself to be a fool.

He paid for it with his life (see 2 Sam. 4:1–12).

Joab—The Destructiveness of Vengeance

Now when Abner returned to Hebron, Joab took him aside into an inner chamber, as if to speak with him privately. And there, to avenge the blood of his brother Asahel, Joab stabbed him in the stomach, and he died. . . . (Joab and his brother Abishai murdered Abner because he had killed their brother Asahel in the battle at Gibeon.)

—2 Samuel 3:27, 30

Joab represents vengeance. For years, he had carried his anger around for losing his brother in battle. The loss of a brother is undoubtedly devastating, but carrying around that kind of anger is destructive to you and everyone around you. By seeking to avenge a wrong committed against his family, Joab damaged the overall fabric of the emerging nation. As in Israel, there are times when the driving forces within us begin to take aim at one another. Jesus recognized this when he said, "No one can serve two masters. Either you will hate the one and love the other, or you will be devoted to the one

and despise the other. You cannot serve both God and money"
(Matt. 6:24). Jesus clearly explained that one person can have
two drives. The drive to earn money is commendable. The
drive to serve God is commendable. When an individual tries
to follow both drives, however, an internal battle is started that
will end in blood. One will overtake the other. David, as Israel's
king, had two military commanders willing to serve him. By that
time, Abner was willing to simply give Ish-Bosheth over to him
without a battle, but he could hardly be trusted. At the same time,
Joab had been loyal and faithful, but carried an angry grudge.
In the end, one killed the other. In the same way, anger can kill
forgiveness. Greed can kill generosity. Fear can kill joy. Hate can
kill love. You cannot live your life like that. Vengeance does not
belong to you. It clearly belongs to the Lord (see Rom. 12:19).

Instead of all of this internal conflict and death, we can
make another choice. By the cleansing blood of Jesus and the
power of the Holy Spirit within us, we can choose to forgive
even when forgiveness is not deserved.

The hurt is real—and it's killing you.

The anger is real—and it's killing you.

The injustice is real—and it's killing you.

The God-given power to forgive is just as real—and it
brings life.

So the internal war rages—but through Jesus' forgiveness
and the Holy Spirit's power, we can allow God to win the war,
and in doing so, conquer our own lives.

PART 3

A HEART OF GRACE

One of the defining characteristics of a great leader, or just a great person for that matter, is a heart filled with grace. Grace is unmerited favor, or, in other words, forgiveness we don't deserve—and can never earn. In King David, we see many examples of this kind of grace, lived out by David himself. In seeing David's application of grace in his life, we can learn how to live grace out in our own lives.

We also will see grace applied by God. We know how to give grace because we have been given grace. It is God's gift of grace that teaches us how to give that gift to others. A godly heart will develop within us a courageous heart, and that heart will ultimately learn to give and receive grace—especially when it isn't deserved.

14

Grace for Those Who Do Not Help

While David was in the wilderness, he heard that Nabal was shearing sheep. So he sent ten young men and said to them, "Go up to Nabal at Carmel and greet him in my name. Say to him: 'Long life to you. Good health to you and your household! And good health to all that is yours! '"Now I hear that it is sheep-shearing time. When your shepherds were with us, we did not mistreat them, and the whole time they were at Carmel nothing of theirs was missing. Ask your own servants and they will tell you. Therefore be favorable toward my men, since we come at a festive time. Please give your servants and your son David whatever you can find for them.'" When David's men arrived, they gave Nabal this message in David's name. Then they waited. Nabal answered David's servants, "Who is this David? Who is this son of Jesse? Many servants are breaking away from their masters these days. Why should I take my bread and water, and the meat I have slaughtered for my shearers, and give it to men coming from who knows where?"

—1 Samuel 25:4–11

Ok, so here is the simple overview of this story. While they were in Carmel, David and his men had protected the shepherds of a man named Nabal. While they were ruthless with their enemies, David's men had a consistent practice of protecting innocent people affected by battles. The time had come for Nabal to shear his sheep, which meant he had an excess of meat and money. In other words, Nabal had plenty to be generous with—and reason to do so—yet he chose not to show generosity to David and his men. Instead, he insulted David by saying, "Who is this David?" Then he brought David's family into it: "Who is this son of Jesse?" Then, with an angry jab, he accused David of insubordination toward King Saul. "Many servants are breaking away from their masters these days." This accusation must have been particularly painful to David, who had given up so much in his attempt to honor God's anointed king. Yet this angry, greedy man was accusing him of something of which he was not guilty.

Now, you may want to give Nabal the benefit of the doubt and assume that he didn't know that Samuel had anointed David as king or that David had refused to kill Saul, even though Saul was trying to kill David. You may want to assume that Nabal was questioning whether the messengers were from David at all.

Those assumptions would be wrong. Nabal knew all of it.

Ancient culture dictated that David could not allow this kind of rudeness to go unchecked. If he did, there would be no help for him and his men anywhere they went from that point on. If David had not dealt with Nabal in a decisive way, he would have been viewed as weak, and no one wanted a weak king. So David had to act against Nabal. His actions were swift, decisive, and potentially deadly. "David said to his men, 'Each of you strap on your sword.' So they did, and David strapped his on as well" (1 Sam. 25:13). David and about four hundred men headed off to deal with Nabal. This was not going to end well for the shepherd from Carmel.

However, Nabal's wife, Abigail, was wise. When she heard what Nabal had done to David, she gathered together as many supplies and gifts as she could and took her servants to meet David and his men. She offered the supplies and gifts, and pled with David not to shed the innocent blood of her household simply because of the foolishness of her husband. "Please pay no attention, my lord, to that wicked man Nabal. He is just like his name—his name means Fool, and folly goes with him" (1 Sam. 25:25). So David relented, took the offering from Abigail, and left Nabal, the fool, and his household alone.

Our modern mind-set could cause us to miss the grace that was extended in this incident. Nabal's insult toward David was a challenge to his authority, courage, and honor. If David did not respond by killing Nabal and his household, he risked losing credibility. If that had happened, he and his men would have faced an endless stream of attacks from other cities, militias, or family clans. So when Abigail approached David and begged for mercy for her household and family, David could have easily refused. Most would have expected him to reject her pleas and continue with his mission to take down anyone who would dare come against him.

He didn't.

David chose to show grace, and it was clearly his choice. By ancient standards, Nabal had committed a crime worthy of death, and Abigail had offered no sufficient defense for his actions. Being a fool does not gain favor with someone you have foolishly made your enemy. So the grace extended to Abigail, and thereby to Nabal, was extended from David's heart, even though Nabal didn't deserve it. That is the very definition of grace—unmerited favor, kindness that is not deserved. A forgiveness that is not deserved. In the Christian understanding of grace, this account is spot on. Nabal was extended favor that he did not deserve as a result of the sacrifice of someone else who loved him, even though he did not deserve her love. Abigail, in her wisdom, saved the day. David, in his kindness, showed mercy. God, however, didn't.

Then in the morning, when Nabal was sober, his wife told him all these things, and his heart failed him and he became like a stone. About ten days later, the LORD struck Nabal and he died.

—1 Samuel 25:37–38

After Nabal's death, Abigail became David's wife. She and the rest of her household spent the remainder of their lives in safety and comfort.

The lesson here is really quite simple. A lack of generosity during a time of plenty is foolish. Some may say that when times are good, you need to hang on to what you have and keep yourself in first place. "Take care of number one." The problem with this mentality is that it disregards and disrespects those who have helped you get where you are today. Think about it. If David and his men had not protected Nabal's servants and flocks on the fields of Carmel, he would have had no sheep to shear. He would not have had servants to feed. He would have had nothing, but he didn't see that. His foolishness blinded him to the thankfulness that should have been at the center of his thinking. His foolishness blinded him to the grace that he should have shown.

I see that occur far too often.

God does not give us things to hoard for ourselves without regard for others. He expects us to be wise and have enough stored up for our own safety, but he also expects us to be generous with what he has given us. Abigail realized this. She understood that the one Nabal had shown disrespect to was capable of taking away everything they had, leaving only destruction and death behind.

Nabal showed stinginess, arrogance, and greed—and that was foolish.

Abigail showed generosity and humility—and that was wise.

David showed grace—and that was kind.

So, how are you going to respond?

15

Grace for Those Who Hurt

So David and Abishai went to the army by night, and there was Saul, lying asleep inside the camp with his spear stuck in the ground near his head. Abner and the soldiers were lying around him. Abishai said to David, "Today God has delivered your enemy into your hands. Now let me pin him to the ground with one thrust of the spear; I won't strike him twice." But David said to Abishai, "Don't destroy him. Who can lay a hand on the Lord's anointed and be guiltless? As surely as the Lord lives," he said, "the Lord himself will strike him, or his time will come and he will die, or he will go into battle and perish. But the Lord forbid that I should lay a hand on the Lord's anointed. Now get the spear and the water jug that are near his head, and let's go."

—1 Samuel 26:7–11

Here we go again. David had another opportunity to kill a helpless Saul, and instead he chose to let him live. To be honest, David's men had to be getting a little tired of this song and dance. They were serving the future king, and yet for some reason, he wouldn't take the opportunities given to him to get the throne. They were living in caves and fields, when they could be back home living in relative peace and security, if David would just kill Saul. Instead, they were spending their lives running from a madman.

What was wrong with David?

Nothing was wrong with David. David simply had a different perspective than his men did on who King Saul was and what he represented. To them, King Saul was nothing more than a madman who stood between them and the life of power and privilege they expected once David was king. With that perspective, they simply could not get rid of King Saul quickly enough.

But David saw something different.

David saw the anointing of God on the head of Saul. It was that anointing from God that made Saul king. God chose him. That is literally what the anointing meant. If God had chosen Saul to be king, who was David to try to unchoose him?

David also saw a man in great pain. I once had a mentor share with me his prayer for my life. "Mike, I am praying that the Holy Spirit will move so powerfully in your life that you simply cannot keep up." I thought that was a pretty mean prayer. Then he continued, "Because once you experience the moving of the Holy Spirit at that level, you will never be satisfied with anything less." OK, now that makes sense. That is what King Saul was wrestling with at this point in his life. He was accustomed to the Spirit of God moving in his life, and now the Spirit of God was missing. He was miserable. He was in agony. And yet he still served as king. He didn't want to let go of the job, but he no longer had the power and leading of the Holy Spirit to accomplish it. So David saw a man in great pain and took pity on him.

Finally, David saw a man whose greatness could live on through his children, and he did not want to do anything that would endanger them. David showed kindness to Saul's descendants even after his death. He did so to honor Jonathan, King Saul's son and David's closest and most trusted friend. David saw in King Saul more than his men were able to see, and as a result, he chose to show grace.

That choice was important for another reason. David understood something that is hard for most people to grasp and yet so important that we are going to look at it once again. God has a timetable and there are no shortcuts to a life of greatness.

Let's look at two distinct boundaries that must exist if we are going to take the full journey from a life filled with promise, where David was, to a life marked by greatness, where David would be.

Don't let circumstances compromise convictions.

In order for our lives to progress the way God intends, we must realize that not all opportunities are God-given or Spirit-led. We will be faced with a multitude of opportunities. Some of them truly are from God. These God-given moments open doors of massive opportunity, progress, effectiveness, and joy. However, not every opportunity is of God. There also will be many opportunities that look promising, even enticing, on the surface, but underneath lies a dark side waiting to steal all the joy.

As I have served the past few decades as a pastor of a growing congregation, I have learned that there is no lack of opportunity. The question is always about the wisdom of the opportunities that present themselves. What looks like a great opportunity could be nothing more than a distraction. We have had many opportunities to open various types of ministries that look great on the surface and have wonderful long-term value. However, when we consider them in light of what God has called us to do, they are revealed to be little more than a distraction. While they may be perfectly right for someone else, they would be a complete failure for us. For instance, people quite often ask me when New Life is going to open a Christian school. My answer is always the same: "I think that would be a great idea for the next pastor." Simply put, I am not called to be the founder of a Christian school. While that may be a great opportunity for someone else and may actually be the center point of God's vision for that person's life, it would be a massive distraction for me. God has not called me to do that. He has called me to be an evangelist and to grow the size and number of churches in the area that he opens up to us. That calling does not involve the day-to-day operations of running a school.

The real art form here is knowing the difference between a God-given opportunity and a distraction. The best I can give you is this: *always, always, always* remember what God's call is on your life and remain true to that. If you don't, you'll start chasing opportunities that look good on the surface, but will cause you heartache in the long run.

Don't let impatience turn into imprudence.

The call on David's life was to be the King of Israel, the nation of God. How is it that the man who was called and anointed to lead God's people could begin his career by stealing the throne and killing the man God anointed before him? That just doesn't sound like a man after God's own heart. If, in this moment, David had allowed his impatience to get the best of him, he would have begun his reign in entirely the wrong way and set himself up for heartache and failure in the long term. You would think that David had to be getting impatient. He was human, after all. He had to remember, and so must we, that God has a timetable. While that timetable is almost never what we wish, it is God's timing and therefore the best timing. To trump God's timetable would lead to a pattern of impatience that would cause a pattern of imprudence in decision-making. Impatience almost always leads to dishonesty, shortcuts, poor quality, and weak integrity.

That was not the king God called David to be.

That is not the person God has called you to be.

16

Grace for Those Who Help

*Then David came to the two hundred men who had been too exhausted to follow him and who were left behind at the Besor Valley. They came out to meet David and the men with him. As David and his men approached, he asked them how they were. But all the evil men and troublemakers among David's followers said, "Because they did not go out with us, we will not share with them the plunder we recovered. However, each man may take his wife and children and go." David replied, "No, my brothers, you must not do that with what the L*ord* has given us. He has protected us and delivered into our hands the raiding party that came against us. Who will listen to what you say? The share of the man who stayed with the supplies is to be the same as that of him who went down to the battle. All will share alike." David made this a statute and ordinance for Israel from that day to this. When David reached Ziklag, he sent some of the plunder to the elders of Judah, who were his friends, saying, "Here is a gift for you from the plunder of the L*ord*'s enemies."*

—1 Samuel 30:21–26

David and his men were facing the first challenge that threatened to divide them and set them against each other. David and his men had returned to their home base in the town of Ziklag. When they arrived, they found that the Amalekites, a rival group, had raided the town and carried off all their wives, children, and possessions, and had burned the town. As you might imagine, great mourning erupted. The men were devastated. Some of them even began talking about stoning David to death. Put it all together. They had been fighting for this man who refused to kill the insane king, who stood between them and a new national order, and his hesitance had cost them their families and possessions.

It did not look good for David.

So, David prayed. God told him to pursue the Amalekites because he was going to catch them, overtake them, and get all of his people and possessions back. David called his men back into fighting order and off they went to chase the Amalekites. Remember, they had just returned from a battle and hadn't had time to rest. They were exhausted and needed to start a new march, and this one needed to move quickly. After traveling for a while, two hundred of David's men become so exhausted that they had to be left behind. With only four hundred men, David pursued the Amalekites. When they caught up to them, they fought for an entire day "from dusk until the evening of the next day," and in the end, "David recovered everything the Amalekites had taken" (1 Sam. 30:17–18).

When they returned to the two hundred who had been too exhausted to continue, the trouble started again. The unity of David's men had already been challenged by loss and grief. Now, the unity of this group of warriors would be challenged again, this time by greed. David faced a decision that would have implications in Jewish law from this point forward. Did the men who stayed with the supplies deserve an equal share in the plunder? David's answer was yes. Remember that in this particular case, the plunder that was taken from the Amalekites was largely the stolen property of the army of David. Therefore, what these men were dividing was largely their own stuff. While some of it was obviously easy to divide—each man may take his wife and children—the rest was not so simple (see 1 Sam. 30:22). David decided that they would split it equally between all of them. Much can be learned from this act of fairness. Let's look at just three simple practices.

Honor those serving under me.

The men who stayed with the supplies had served the men who went off to battle. The lesson had already been learned: Don't leave your stuff unprotected or someone will steal it. So while the men guarding the supplies did so because they were exhausted, they also provided an important service to the men who were fighting. They didn't have to worry about the security of their families and stuff back at Besor Valley while they fought. They could fight on the front lines knowing that their home base was safe. This kind of service had to be honored because it was vitally important. Whether we serve in a military, a business, a church, or a home, the truth is that there are those who serve us. Some of them we see clearly, such as the military, police, and first responders. Some we hardly even notice, such as the trash collectors, sewage plant employees, and janitors. Yet all of them are vitally important. If the employees at the sewage plant would all quit their jobs, we would soon realize how important their service really was. If the trash collectors all stopped picking up our trash, we would miss their important service. So the lesson is simple and clear. There are no unimportant jobs, even when evil men and troublemakers act like there are (see 1 Sam. 30:22).

Honor those serving with me.

David addressed those who wanted to withhold the plunder from those who stayed behind by saying, "No, my brothers." Even though the Bible clearly calls them "evil men and troublemakers," David referred to them as brothers (see 1 Sam. 30:22–23). David was also careful not to disrespect those who were fighting beside him while he insisted on respecting those who stayed back to serve. This is an important balance to strike. All too often when we insist on honoring everyone, we unintentionally fail to honor those who have paid the greatest price. Parents, teachers, childcare workers, cooks, and janitorial staff sometimes fall into this category. We know that we need these folks. We know that they are always right beside us, loving us, training us, nurturing us, feeding us, and keeping us safe, but somehow we forget to honor them. Maybe it is because they are always there. Since they are never away from us, but always serving right beside us, perhaps we forget to honor them. When we do that, we make a horrible mistake. They are always there, they fight alongside us, they defend our vulnerabilities, and they cover our backs. We must not forget to honor those who serve with us.

Honor those serving around me.

There is one other group to remember when sharing in praise and honor. There are those who support you and are your friends from a distance. For whatever reason, they cannot or will not join you on the field of battle this time, but history has shown them to be loyal and valuable friends. Like the security guard on the college campus or the EMT arriving on the ambulance, we never see these folks until their presence is imperative. They seem to disappear into the very fabric of the society we live in until we need them. All the time they are out of our sight, they are training, watching, studying, and preparing for that one moment when their practice and preparation will save our lives. Never forget to honor them. It will matter in the long run.

Very soon, David would be working to unify the kingdom of Israel under his leadership, and his thoughtfulness here likely helped pave the way to that transition (see 1 Sam. 30:26).

Smart.

17

Grace for Those Who Precede Me

Then David and all the men with him took hold of their clothes and tore them. They mourned and wept and fasted till evening for Saul and his son Jonathan, and for the army of the LORD and for the nation of Israel, because they had fallen by the sword.

—2 Samuel 1:11–12

King Saul is dead.

David had predicted it would happen this way. There was no real surprise in this moment; everyone knew it was coming. Even when there is no surprise in death, there is still pain. As David and his men heard of the horrible defeat at the hands of the Philistines, they remembered that the army that was defeated was an army of their brothers, their countrymen, and their family. It was Israel that lost on that battlefield. The God-anointed King Saul led the Israelite army who lost that day. This defeat was complete. Most of the sons of Saul, at least the ones in immediate line for the throne, were killed in battle. The most disturbing loss for David was the loss of his best friend, Jonathan.

Everything had changed.

Everyone knew it.

David was about to become king. He knew this, and so did everyone around him. With some notable exceptions, there would be little resistance throughout Israel to the establishment of the new order of things. Everyone knew that Saul was insane, and most likely they were ready to move on. David, once again, understood the importance of grace and honor.

Honestly, in our modern American culture, we have largely lost this sense of honor for those who are our elders or those who have gone before us. We lack an understanding of history and its importance, and we seem to have little concern for anything that is more than, say, two minutes old. This culture of the immediate over the important is not healthy. If you are living in this mind-set, let me give you a few reminders.

There is no glory in gloating.

David had won. There was no getting around that. Saul had sought to kill David for years, and he had committed tremendous amounts of time and resources to that effort. Now Saul was dead, and David would sit on the throne that Saul had been trying to protect. Though David had won, there would be no gloating. Instead, there would be mourning. There would be a sincere display of sorrow over the great loss on that battlefield, and David would lead it.

I must tell you that our cultural practice of gloating is unseemly, ugly, and destructive. When I watch athletes, politicians, entertainers or any group that has somehow risen to the top of their field act in arrogance and insolence, it makes me sick. Gloating is ugly, and it is not of God. Had David held some victory party at Saul's death, some would have been more than happy to join in the celebration. They would have been honored to stand next to the new king and take smiling selfies to post on their social media pages. It would have been great fun.

What message would have been sent to the families of the honorable soldiers who died with Saul? What message would have been sent to the grieving family of Jonathan and his brothers who had nothing to do with their father's insane rampage the past few years? What message would have been sent to the nation that needed to heal and somehow come back together?

Gloating makes enemies.

Gloating shows extreme shallowness.

Gloating is never a good idea.

Gloating is not godly.

There is no winning in losing.

Keep in mind that every time someone wins, someone else loses. For every person who is celebrating, there is someone who is mourning. Israel had lost her king in a horrible manner. Israel had lost many valiant warriors. The enemy of Israel had been emboldened and would likely attack again. While this might have felt like a victory to those few brave men who had been following David all along, it surely felt like a devastating loss to the rest of the kingdom.

There is no future in forgetting.

History is important, even the darker parts of it. When history is forgotten, it is tragically repeated. To forget the journey that brought us to where we are is to place our progress and existence in jeopardy. Whether we are talking about our planet, nation, state, county, city, family, marriage, children, or selves, history is ignored to our own peril. If you don't remember how you got to where you are today, then you will forget the pitfalls that almost took you down the first time around, and perhaps you will fall into them again. So remember the good days, the bad days, the ugly days, and the "whatever" days. Remember and give honor where honor is due, and grace where grace is needed.

18

Grace for Those Who Love

*David asked, "Is there anyone still left of the house of
Saul to whom I can show kindness for Jonathan's sake?"*
—2 Samuel 9:1

David had established himself as king over all of Israel (see
2 Sam. 5:1–3). It is often interesting to see what oppressed
people do when they move into positions of power. Sometimes
the power proves to be too much for them, and the oppressed
simply become the new oppressors. However, once in a while,
you get a leader who is made of something more. Once in
power, David could have chosen to do anything he desired
with his power, wealth, and time. Yet he thought about others
rather than himself. David thought about God and the fact that
God's worship was still taking place in a tent. David yearned
to build a temple for his God. He yearned to use his power,
influence, and wealth to the glory of his God. This is a man
who was made of something more. Then, David began to look
for someone of Saul's house to show kindness to, in order to
honor his friend Jonathan.

What David found was pure gold.

David found that there was a son of Jonathan still alive. His name was Mephibosheth. (Yeah, try giving your kid that name.) Through a former servant of Saul named Ziba, David found Mephibosheth and brought him to Jerusalem. Mephibosheth had been living in Lo Debar. Now, we know almost nothing about Lo Debar, but the word translates as "no pasture." So, let me speculate and say that Mephibosheth lived in a place with a lousy economy and little to attract anyone to visit. I imagine Lo Debar was a dry, barren place where there was little hope and little beauty.

David called Mephibosheth out of "no pasture" to the palace.

No doubt Mephibosheth was nervous about this meeting. First, he was a direct descendent of the former king and therefore had a legitimate claim to the throne. To an insecure king, this would have made him a potential threat. Fortunately for Mephibosheth, David was not insecure. Second, Mephibosheth was crippled. His feet had been injured as a child while the family was escaping after the death of Saul and Jonathan (see 2 Sam. 4:4). So, if the king wanted some type of productive work out of Mephibosheth, it wasn't going to happen. In fact, Mephibosheth gives us insight into how he viewed himself in his response to David's declaration of why he had been summoned: "What is your servant, that you should notice a dead dog like me?" (2 Sam. 9:8).

Ever felt that way?

Yeah, I think we all have at some point.

When David looked at Mephibosheth, he did not see a dead dog. David saw the son of a beloved friend and he had great plans:

"Don't be afraid," David said to him, "for I will surely show you kindness for the sake of your father Jonathan. I will restore to you all the land that belonged to your grandfather Saul, and you will always eat at my table."

—2 Samuel 9:7

David intended to bless Mephibosheth for the sake of honoring Jonathan. Imagine, in one day, Mephibosheth had gone from languishing and forgotten in Lo Debar to sitting at the king's table as a family member. He had gone from broke to wealthy and from powerless to powerful.

He hadn't done anything to deserve it.

I believe in something called generational blessing. It works like this. Sometimes people find themselves blessed by God, and others based solely on the actions and righteousness of family members that have gone before them. Mephibosheth was only five when his father was killed in battle. He likely remembered next to nothing about his father. Mephibosheth was lame in both feet by no fault of his own. In fact, his life so far had been a tragedy he had done nothing to deserve.

Dead dad. Disability. Bad neighborhood. No money. No way to make money. And none of it was his fault. My guess is that he was pretty bitter. Then the blessings came, and just like the hardships, he did nothing to deserve them.

He was just born into the right family.

I often have wondered why God has been so good to me and my family. I can only attribute it to the godliness and righteousness of my grandfathers. Grandpa Hilson and Grandpa Freeman were both Wesleyan pastors with small congregations. They both labored and toiled to preach and teach the truth of God's Word their entire lives. They were both wonderful men of God. When I look at my life, I cannot help but believe that I have the privilege of living in their blessings. I haven't done anything to deserve such blessings from God. I will likely never be as righteous and holy as they were, and yet I find myself believing that God chooses to bless me and my family in order to show kindness for both of their sakes.

I believe in residual blessings.

Now, you may or may not have a family tree with God-fearing, righteous people in it. That isn't really the point. Your family history does not have to determine your future legacy. Since Jesus paid the price for our sins and the Holy Spirit chooses to live within us, we have been adopted into a new family. Listen to the words of the apostle Paul:

For those who are led by the Spirit of God are the children of God. The Spirit you received does not make you slaves, so that you live in fear again; rather, the Spirit you received brought about your adoption to sonship. And by him we cry, "Abba [daddy], Father." The Spirit himself testifies with our spirit that we are God's children.

—Romans 8:14–16

So, your new family tree begins with Abraham and includes Jesus. That's a pretty impressive heritage.

That kind of heritage comes with responsibility. At this point, it is your job to become a Jonathan to your kids and grandkids, who are represented in this story by Mephibosheth. Think of it this way. If I am being blessed for the commitment and righteousness of my grandfathers, then it stands to reason that I can (and should) live my life in such a way as to draw down blessings to my children and their children.

So, that becomes my goal. That becomes the lens through which I view my world and make my decisions. I don't make decisions based solely on what will make me happy or bring me temporary fun. I make choices based on what will work in the long run to establish a legacy that my children and grandchildren can be blessed by. I want to leave them in the best place possible with the most blessings possible.

Look, we cannot control the events of our children's lives. Hard times may overtake them. Others may hurt them and leave them traumatized, physically or emotionally. What we can control is the legacy we leave behind for them. If our legacy is strong enough, then the blessing of that legacy can overcome any struggle they may face. Lo Debar will not hold them down if we have spent our lives lifting them up. Broken feet will not keep them trapped if we have spent our lives being a blessing. Any darkness that enters their existence will be temporary.

What I describe may or may not be your current reality. In fact, it may be virtually the opposite of what I am describing. It's not too late to start. It's never too late to start.

Brothers and sisters, I do not consider myself yet to have taken hold of it [the righteousness of Christ]. But one thing I do: Forgetting what is behind and straining toward what is ahead, I press on toward the goal to win the prize for which God has called me heavenward in Christ Jesus.

—Philippians 3:13–14

So, if a godly legacy is already your goal—keep it up. If a godly legacy has not been your goal—get started.

19

Grace for Those Who Curse

As King David approached Bahurim, a man from the same clan as Saul's family came out from there. His name was Shimei son of Gera, and he cursed as he came out. He pelted David and all the king's officials with stones, though all the troops and the special guard were on David's right and left. As he cursed, Shimei said, "Get out, get out, you murderer, you scoundrel. The LORD has repaid you for all the blood you shed in the household of Saul, in whose place you have reigned. The LORD has given the kingdom into the hands of your son Absalom. You have come to ruin because you are a murderer." Then Abishai son of Zeruiah said to the king, "Why should this dead dog curse my lord the king? Let me go over and cut off his head." But the king said, "What does this have to do with you, you sons of Zeruiah? If he is cursing because the LORD said to him, 'Curse David,' who can ask, 'Why do you do this?'" David then said to Abishai and all his officials, "My son, my own flesh and blood, is trying to kill me. How much more, then, this Benjamite. Leave him alone; let him curse, for the LORD has told him to. It may be that the LORD will look upon my misery and restore to me his covenant blessing instead of his curse today."

—2 Samuel 16:5–12

Perhaps you have noticed that David seems to have developed a much darker, more defeated attitude? A lot has transpired that we will deal with in detail later, but let me sum it up for the sake of understanding this particular passage.

David's life was lived in two sections. There is David BB and David AB. The line of delineation is Bathsheba. Before Bathsheba (BB), David's life seemed so completely blessed that it was almost magical. This is what happens when you are deeply devoted to God's ways and God's truth. Then at some point, David began making choices based on his own desires rather than God's. He slept with another man's wife, Bathsheba (AB). He killed Uriah, Bathsheba's husband. He took Bathsheba to be his own wife, all the while trying to hide his own sin. While God forgave David of this sinful period in his life, things were just never the same. David had more trouble in the kingdom. His kids turned out to be a mess. One of his own sons, Absalom, took over the palace and attempted to replace David as king.

David seems to have been so broken by that time that he didn't even put up a fight.

David was on the road, being cursed at and pelted with stones by some local who was accusing him of things he hadn't done. That's a long, hard fall from cloud nine.

David showed grace.

He could have allowed Abishai to kill Shimei, but he didn't. David understood something about himself that all the others with him could not possibly have known.

He deserved this treatment.

Shimei accused David of killing off the household of King Saul when David had done no such thing. In fact, he made a specific point not to do that. So Shimei was cursing David for something David hadn't done. But, David had done plenty enough to deserve to be cursed. He had failed as a husband, and to cover it up, killed Uriah, Bathsheba's husband. He had failed as a father, and his kids were killing each other. One of his sons, Absalom, was even trying to kill him. He had failed as a leader, and all of his officials and soldiers were once again on the run. He had failed as king, and his nation was in turmoil. He was convinced that he had failed as a man. He honestly never came to the place where he was willing to personally deal with Absalom and restore his kingdom.

Did you catch all of that?

David was convinced he was a failure.

It was at least partially true. He really had failed at all of those things. However, having failed, even multiple times, does not make one a failure, although it may feel like it. Sometimes you just know that you deserve a good, solid cussing out. Sometimes you are convinced that God himself has sent the cusser to do the cussin'. You hear all kinds of truth in those cuss words.

God is still forgiving.

David would regain his throne. He would endure the death of his son, Absalom, and the natural struggles that come with an aging leader. God would restore him. Truth is, life isn't always magical. Those wonderful moments that seem so magically blessed should be savored with the knowledge that not all of life's moments are like that. There will come a day when you will get cussed out. You will deserve it. When it comes, take it like a child of God and trust him to restore you. He will always restore you, as long as you trust in him.

God's desire for us is not to destroy us. His desire is to improve us, bless us, lift us up, and give us a future. The nation of Israel rejected God over and over again for literally centuries, and through the prophet Jeremiah, God declared: "For I know the plans I have for you," declares the LORD, "plans to prosper you and not to harm you, plans to give you hope and a future" (Jer. 29:11). If God could have great plans for a nation that had repeatedly rejected him through the centuries, then surely he has great plans for you even though you have messed up.

God would restore David. His pain would ease but never leave. He would never forget what he had done and the misery it had caused. He would always know that God had restored him anyway. Even when King David gave up on King David, God never did.

God hasn't given up on you either.

20

Grace for Me

Praise the LORD, my soul; all my inmost being, praise his holy name. Praise the LORD, my soul, and forget not all his benefits—who forgives all your sins and heals all your diseases, who redeems your life from the pit and crowns you with love and compassion, who satisfies your desires with good things so that your youth is renewed like the eagle's. The LORD works righteousness and justice for all the oppressed. He made known his ways to Moses, his deeds to the people of Israel: The LORD is compassionate and gracious, slow to anger, abounding in love. He will not always accuse, nor will he harbor his anger forever; he does not treat us as our sins deserve or repay us according to our iniquities. For as high as the heavens are above the earth, so great is his love for those who fear him; as far as the east is from the west, so far has he removed our transgressions from us. As a father has compassion on his children, so the LORD has compassion on those who fear him; for he knows how we are formed, he remembers that we are dust. The life of mortals is like grass, they flourish like a flower of the field; the wind blows over it and it is gone, and its place remembers it no more. But from everlasting to everlasting the LORD's love is with those who fear him, and his righteousness with their children's children—with those who keep his covenant and remember to obey his precepts. The LORD has established his throne in heaven, and his kingdom rules over all. Praise the LORD, you his angels, you mighty ones who do his bidding, who obey his word. Praise the LORD, all his heavenly hosts, you his servants who do his will. Praise the LORD, all his works everywhere in his dominion. Praise the LORD, my soul.

—Psalm 103

As we've noted, King David was a talented musician. He wrote many songs in his lifetime, and many are recorded in the book of Psalms. This one is particularly interesting in our discussion about grace. Let's take a look at three overarching ideas that David establishes for our understanding of God in this psalm.

He is our healer.

God is often seen as big, scary, angry, distant. . . . (You choose a frightening adjective and add it here.) People fail to understand that God is our healer. He heals us physically and spiritually.

Physical healing—Yes, it is true. God does still heal his people physically. Although our modern mind-set views such a belief as ridiculous, it is true nonetheless. God at times chooses to intervene in a physical way. These occurrences may be rare, but they are real.

Spiritual healing—Here is where God intervenes for us on a daily basis. While we tend to see him as frightening and accusing, the truth is very different. The God that David writes about and we still serve to this day "is compassionate and gracious, slow to anger, abounding in love" (Ps. 103:8). He does not always accuse, and he chooses in his own love and grace to not "treat us as our sins deserve" and to ultimately throw our sins as far away from us "as the east is from the west" (Ps. 103:10, 12). When the only one who has the authority to judge you instead chooses to be compassionate and forgiving, you can finally find peace.

He is our helper.

Our God is like a good father to us. He knows us. He gets us. He understands our weaknesses. He remembers "how we are formed" (Ps. 103:14). He understands better than anyone our flaws. He has compassion on us "as a father has compassion on his children" (Ps. 103:13). He understands us.

Those who view God as demanding and exacting, expecting perfection from us on a daily basis, need to take hope in the fact that he "remembers that we are dust" (Ps. 103:14). He never expects perfection out of us, because he knows that we are not capable of perfection. He expects more out of us, because he has forgiven us. He was there when we were created, he understands how weak and vulnerable we are, and he chooses to love us anyway. That is amazing grace. That is the amazing grace of a father.

He is our hope.

In the end, we can trust that God will be there. "From everlasting to everlasting the LORD's love is with those who fear him" (Ps. 103:17). In the beginning, God was there, and in the end, God will still be there. He is the unchanging, undefeated One whom we serve and in whom we find our hope.

So, when you feel like you have failed so badly that God will not forgive, remember he is the God who "forgives all your sins" (Ps. 103:3).

When you feel like you are so broken in your humanity that there is no longer hope of overcoming, remember: "As a father has compassion on his children, so the LORD has compassion on those who fear him" (Ps. 103:13). Or said another way, the Lord has compassion on those who respect and follow him. This verse is not calling us to some paralyzing fear that equates to terror. No, this verse calls us to a level of respect that we would do anything to bring joy to the heart of the One who has earned our respectful obedience.

When you feel the end is near and there is little hope, remember: "The LORD has established his throne in heaven, and his kingdom rules over all" (Ps. 103:19).

God has offered you healing—accept it.

God has offered you help—take it.

God has offered you hope—live in it.

God has offered you grace—so now forgive yourself . . . and move on.

PART 4

A FLAWED HEART

OK, let us start this out right. Everyone has a flawed heart. There are no perfect people and therefore no perfect hearts. God created us with pure, unflawed hearts. When God placed Adam and Eve in the garden of Eden, they were both pure, unflawed humans. As you know, they made choices that messed all of that up. The choice to rebel against God and his simple command sets in motion the sin that now resides in us all and produces flaws in each one of us. Their sin caused our flaws.

Let us be careful here not to fall into a victim mentality. It's true that the original sin committed in the garden of Eden left all of humanity flawed, and none of us were even there. So it is true that we are living in the fallout of someone else's screwup. Let's just not get too high and mighty. Every one of us has made our own flawed choices.

In the end, the flaw is not the point. It's just there. Yes, the flaws in our hearts cause sin. Yes, sin causes more flaws in our hearts. Here is the point that I want you to find in the following set of accounts from the life of David: even though sin can sometimes have devastating consequences, God is willing and able to provide forgiveness and healing.

That is the point here. You have sinned. You have screwed up. You have a flawed heart. God is in the business of fixing and redeeming flawed hearts.

21

A Heart That Wanders

In the spring, at the time when kings go off to war, David sent Joab out with the king's men and the whole Israelite army. They destroyed the Ammonites and besieged Rabbah. But David remained in Jerusalem.

—2 Samuel 11:1

This event marks a turning point in the life of King David—and it's not a good one. In fact, this story gives us great warning and great hope. When God rejected King Saul, he said this through Samuel the prophet in speaking of Saul's successor, David: "The LORD has sought out a man after his own heart and appointed him ruler of his people" (1 Sam. 13:14). The apostle Paul repeated this statement in Acts 13:22: "God testified concerning him: 'I have found David son of Jesse, a man after my own heart; he will do everything I want him to do.'" Yet David was a deeply flawed man. He took Bathsheba, the wife of Uriah, and had his way with her while her husband was out fighting for the nation and for the king. It's hard to imagine a deeper betrayal. He not only violated

Uriah's marriage, he disrespected someone who was off risking his life for him. Then he intentionally placed Uriah in a part of the battle where he would certainly die. A warrior was disrespected and then murdered by his own king. This was deeply flawed.

We are getting ahead of ourselves.

First, let's consider the hope that can be found in this dark moment in David's life. There is hope to be found in the fact that God is not looking for perfect people to lead his kingdom. David was obviously not perfect. In fact, what we see of him in this incident would disqualify him from leadership in almost any country, business, organization, or community today. David really messed up. But God chose him anyway. How do we unpack that? Consider this statement: It is possible for a person to act, for a time, in a manner that is inconsistent with his heart, but it is impossible for a person to act, for a lifetime, in a manner that is inconsistent with his heart.

I believe that to be a true statement. David was a man after God's own heart, but something caused him to act, for a time, in a manner that was grossly inconsistent with his godly heart. So, take hope in the fact that God does not demand perfection in our actions; he wants surrender in our hearts.

Now comes the warning. Though God did not reject David, there was a high cost to his actions. David's life would never again be as effective and productive. The time he spent acting in a manner that was inconsistent with his heart would cause pain for David, in one way or another, for the rest of his life. Sin does this to us. While we may find true forgiveness from

God for our sins, that forgiveness does not negate the consequences of our sinful choices. There is always a price to pay. Sin is never free of charge.

With all of that in mind, let's take some time and consider where David went wrong. In doing so, perhaps we can avoid the pain and loss of effectiveness that comes with sinful choices. We will look at four ways that David went wrong and consider how we can avoid these pitfalls in our own lives. As we look at them, let's set boundaries that act as guardrails. Then let's allow these guardrails to help us stay on the right road and not wreck our lives in the ditches of poor judgment.

Boundary 1—Keep your heart in the work.

In the spring, at the time when kings go off to war, David sent Joab out with the king's men and the whole Israelite army. They destroyed the Ammonites and besieged Rabbah. But David remained in Jerusalem.

—2 Samuel 11:1

David was not where he was supposed to be. For some reason, and we don't really know why, he decided to stay in Jerusalem, while Joab, his general, and the king's army went off to war. This was not normal. In those days, kings went off to fight with their armies. David was basically calling in sick to work, and others were doing his work for him. This simple act gives us our first indication that David was acting in a manner that was inconsistent with the way his heart had led him prior to this point in his life. He had never let his men down before . . . but here he did.

Now, David's real failure was not in skipping work. The real failure was the trouble he got into when he had all of that newfound free time. You likely have heard the phrase "Idle hands are the devil's workshop" (Prov. 16:27 TLB). This is a true warning. When you allow yourself to lose discipline in one area of your life, that loss of discipline will begin to affect other areas. David wasn't at war; instead, he was on the roof of the palace. Since Uriah *was* at war, faithfully living out his responsibility, Bathsheba was alone. If David had been where he was supposed to be, he would have been fighting beside Uriah. Instead, he was lying beside Uriah's wife. David was out of God's will and out of his place. Not that there is anything wrong with taking a day off from work once in a while. However, this was more than that. David refused to be where he knew he should be. In a flawed heart, that kind of rebellion opened the door to deeper failures and sins.

The lesson is really simple. Be where you are supposed to be, do what you are supposed to do, and don't let your free time become the devil's workplace.

Boundary 2—Keep your eyes on the work.

One evening David got up from his bed and walked around on the roof of the palace. From the roof he saw a woman bathing. The woman was very beautiful.

—2 Samuel 11:2

You see the problem here, don't you? David was not where he was supposed to be, and he then began looking at stuff he was not supposed to see. I don't think this was the first time David had seen this woman bathing. Though the Bible doesn't tell us this, I think it is likely that she was part of the reason he didn't go off to war in the first place. I also think that he knew what time to go out on his roof and see her there. However, since the Bible doesn't tell us, let us give David the benefit of the doubt and say he accidentally looked out and saw Bathsheba. David was randomly walking around on the roof of his palace and—oops. He looked over and saw a really pretty lady bathing.

Now, pause.

David had a choice in this moment. He could have simply looked away, gotten off the roof, and left her alone . . . or . . . he could have stood there staring. He obviously chose to stare. He had to know this was inappropriate. He should not have been watching this woman, who was not his wife and was someone else's wife. He should have repented of his actions right then and went back downstairs to take a cold shower.

Our eyes do that sort of thing to us. When we spend too much time looking at what we have no business looking at, it starts to affect our thinking, emotions, and morals. As our eyes focus on the unhealthy, our minds begin to reason away the sinfulness of sin. David was probably thinking, *Well, I am king, after all. Everything in the kingdom technically belongs to me. I'm not actually going to take her from Uriah; I will just borrow her for a night or two while he is away. Nobody will get hurt. It will be fine.*

So his thinking was obviously skewed, but sin never works that way. Sin always hurts, always destroys; and, sooner or later, sin is always found out.

Keeping your eyes where they belong will help you keep your mind where it belongs, your morals where they belong, and your hands where they belong. This brings us to the next boundary.

Boundary 3—Keep your hands to yourself.

David sent someone to find out about her. The man said, "She is Bathsheba, the daughter of Eliam and the wife of Uriah the Hittite." Then David sent messengers to get her. She came to him, and he slept with her.

—2 Samuel 11:3–4

Poor thinking, caused by not keeping his hands at his work and his eyes to himself, led David to poor actions. Look, this sinfulness was progressively getting worse. It all started with being lazy and not going to work where he belonged. Then it progressed to staring longingly at someone who didn't belong to him. Then he started thinking about her. He asked about her. He researched her. He started stalking and following her social media posts. (Well, he would if he were around today.) The thinking likely turned into obsession, and then he acted on it. Now, it's true that in David's case, all of this progressed very quickly. Unless he had been looking at Bathsheba for a long time, all of this happened in one night. That kind of rapid decline is possible and common. That is why these boundaries are so important. It doesn't take long to wreck your integrity and righteousness on the side of life's road, especially when you have let all the boundaries down.

When you let yourself be somewhere you shouldn't be, see things you shouldn't see, think about things you shouldn't be thinking about, it's not long before you do things you shouldn't do. That is where life gets all messed up. Listen, it was not good for David to stay home while his army went to fight, but that was not the sin. It was not good for David to see Bathsheba from the roof, but, at first sight, that was not a sin. Choosing to stare at her was where the sin started. Choosing to keep thinking about her was where the sin grew. Sending for her was where the sin became full-grown. Listen to the words of James on this matter:

Each person is tempted when they are dragged away by their own evil desire and enticed. Then, after desire has conceived, it gives birth to sin; and sin, when it is full-grown, gives birth to death.

—James 1:14–15

That is exactly the pattern David experienced. It is the same pattern we will experience if we don't keep the boundaries in place. But it was about to get worse for David.

Boundary 4—Keep your integrity, no matter what.

The woman conceived and sent word to David, saying,
"I am pregnant."

—2 Samuel 11:5

When David realized that Bathsheba was pregnant, he
knew his secret would get out. So he devised a plan to hide
his sin. He sent word to Joab to bring Uriah home so that he
could sleep with Bathsheba and everyone would think Uriah
was the father. But Uriah was a man of great honor, and he
would not sleep with his wife while his brothers were sleeping
in tents and fighting for their lives.

Uriah said to David, "The ark and Israel and Judah are
staying in tents, and my commander Joab and my lord's
men are camped in the open country. How could I go to
my house to eat and drink and make love to my wife?
As surely as you live, I will not do such a thing."

—2 Samuel 11:11

Those words must have struck David like a dagger. The very thing that Uriah was refusing to do was what David had been doing all along. The ark, Israel, Judah, and Joab's and David's men had been in the open fields for some time. David had been at home eating, drinking, and sleeping—with Bathsheba. When you are failing to be a person of integrity and someone of real integrity comes along, it hurts. In the light of their right choices, your wrong ones become glaringly obvious.

David still didn't seem to get it.

David got Uriah drunk and sent him home. However, even a drunk Uriah had more integrity in that moment than a sober King David. "But in the evening Uriah went out to sleep on his mat among his master's servants; he did not go home" (2 Sam. 11:13). When David realized he couldn't make Uriah sleep with Bathsheba, he did the unthinkable. He wrote a letter to Joab and sent it with Uriah.

"Put Uriah out in front where the fighting is fiercest. Then withdraw from him so he will be struck down and die." So while Joab had the city under siege, he put Uriah at a place where he knew the strongest defenders were. When the men of the city came out and fought against Joab, some of the men in David's army fell; moreover, Uriah the Hittite died.

—2 Samuel 11:14–17

David chose to stay home when he belonged somewhere else. David chose to stare when his eyes belonged somewhere else. David chose to take what belonged to someone else.

All of that drove David to murder.

Now, most people will never let poor choices lead them that far astray. Murder is an extreme, but the attempt to hide your sin is always costly and harmful. It always kills something, if only your integrity. Remember what I said earlier? The consequences of confession always pale in comparison to the cost of concealment. True statement.

David could have simply confessed his sin to Uriah and to those in the palace. Certainly that would have been easier than having him killed. In order to avoid the discomfort of telling the truth, David went to all the trouble of sending for Uriah, watching where he slept, throwing a party just to get him drunk, and ultimately having him placed in the battle so that he would be killed. All that trouble just so David wouldn't have to tell the truth.

We often go to great lengths to hide our sin. We work so hard at the lying it takes to cover up the sin that we don't realize how much easier it would be to just tell the truth and repent. Not to mention, we haven't fooled anyone. Think about it. People are not stupid. Uriah must have figured that something wasn't right. The king brought him home and suddenly was interested in his sex life with his wife. You think that didn't register with Uriah? Joab got a request from the king to send Uriah home, and then later, a command to have Uriah killed.

You really think that didn't register with Joab? Then, once Uriah was dead, a quickie wedding at some cheesy chapel in Vegas . . . and then a baby arrives in, say, eight months . . . but nobody knows? Right. How foolish. Let's be honest with ourselves. We are not good at hiding sin.

Sin is really good at being found out.

Honestly, the process of attempting to fake integrity is one of the biggest destroyers of integrity. When we attempt to keep our sins secret, we end up caught in a web of lies and deceit. Secrets breed lies. When those lies are found out, the result is a complete loss of trust and integrity.

22

A Heart That Is Guilty

The LORD sent Nathan to David. When he came to him, he said, "There were two men in a certain town, one rich and the other poor. The rich man had a very large number of sheep and cattle, but the poor man had nothing except one little ewe lamb he had bought. He raised it, and it grew up with him and his children. It shared his food, drank from his cup and even slept in his arms. It was like a daughter to him. Now a traveler came to the rich man, but the rich man refrained from taking one of his own sheep or cattle to prepare a meal for the traveler who had come to him. Instead, he took the ewe lamb that belonged to the poor man and prepared it for the one who had come to him." David burned with anger against the man and said to Nathan, "As surely as the LORD lives, the man who did this must die. He must pay for that lamb four times over, because he did such a thing and had no pity."

—2 Samuel 12:1–6

Isn't it amazing how blind we can be to our own sin? David seems to have had no idea that Nathan was setting him up. God had already told the prophet Nathan what David had done. So Nathan set the stage for a confrontation. David was so blinded by his own wrong thinking that he couldn't see himself in the story. If he had, he would have had the chance to confess. Instead, he just got angry. That seems to be how it works. The folks who are the angriest about a particular type of sin are often the very ones who get caught up in it. They will declare some over-the-top, harsh penalty for others who commit that sin, even though they are just as guilty. David declares that this man must "pay for that lamb four times over" (2 Sam. 12:6).

This brings up a very real life lesson that we should always remember. Be careful how you judge others. Jesus said: "Do not judge, or you too will be judged. For in the same way you judge others, you will be judged, and with the measure you use, it will be measured to you" (Matt. 7:1–2). Do not take this warning lightly. Let me show you something. Let me show you the fourfold path of death and destruction that ran through David's family as result of his sinfulness.

The son who was conceived by David and Bathsheba during their affair died (see 2 Sam. 12:15–19).

David's son, Amnon, raped his half-sister, Tamar, and was killed by his half-brother, Absalom (see 13:1–29).

David's son, Absalom, overthrew David, became king, slept with all of David's wives, and was killed by David's general, Joab (see 15–18).

David's son, Adonijah, was killed by his half-brother, Solomon, when he attempted to become king after the death of David (see 1 Kings 2:25).

Do you see the progression? David unknowingly set the terms of his own punishment. Never allow yourself to become so self-unaware that you attempt to bring unfair judgment to those who are guilty of the same sin as you. Jesus clearly tells us that this is a bad idea (see Matt. 7:2). David made that mistake and it didn't end well.

Then Nathan said to David, "You are the man. This is what the LORD, the God of Israel, says: 'I anointed you king over Israel, and I delivered you from the hand of Saul. I gave your master's house to you, and your master's wives into your arms. I gave you all Israel and Judah. And if all this had been too little, I would have given you even more. Why did you despise the word of the LORD by doing what is evil in his eyes? You struck down Uriah the Hittite with the sword and took his wife to be your own. You killed him with the sword of the Ammonites. Now, therefore, the sword will never depart from your house, because you despised me and took the wife of Uriah the Hittite to be your own.' This is what the LORD says: 'Out of your own household I am going to bring calamity on you. Before your very eyes I will take your wives and give them to

one who is close to you, and he will sleep with your wives in broad daylight. You did it in secret, but I will do this thing in broad daylight before all Israel.'"

—2 Samuel 12:7–12

Did you hear what God had to say? After listing all the things he had given to David, God said, "And if all this had been too little, I would have given you even more" (2 Sam. 12:8). This was a tough lesson to learn, but we need to stop trying to take, in our own power, what God would willingly give us by his generous and loving hand. We need to stop looking at and desiring to have what belongs to our neighbors and start giving God praise for all he has given us. When we focus on what we don't have to the point that we go out and try to get it on our own, we sin and make a mess of our lives. Trust God to give us all we need, and he will give us even more. And never forget:

Sin is never free.

Sin always kills.

The consequences of confession always pale in comparison to the cost of concealment.

Honestly, you will commit sin at some point in your life. We are all human, so it happens. When you do, confess it quickly and work diligently to clean up the mess you have made. God can and will forgive a repentant heart.

23

A Heart That Needs Forgiveness

> Then David said to Nathan, "I have sinned against the LORD." Nathan replied, "The LORD has taken away your sin. You are not going to die. But because by doing this you have shown utter contempt for the LORD, the son born to you will die."
>
> —2 Samuel 12:13–14

God forgives.

The fact that God chooses to forgive us even when we have violated his grace and his law is truly amazing. Consider what we have seen so far in this particular account from the life of David. David failed in his responsibility as king because he refused to go with his army into battle. He failed in his responsibility as a follower of God because he entertained his desire for a woman who was not his to have. He failed in his responsibility as a neighbor by taking his neighbor's wife. He failed in his responsibility as a leader of integrity by attempting to lie his way through his mess. He failed in his responsibility as the commander in chief by intentionally killing one of his own men. So, let us make sure we have it all covered. David is a luster, a liar, a cheat, and a murderer.

God chooses to forgive him.

Wow.

God's forgiveness is undeserved. That is absolutely certain. We have done nothing to earn such elaborate grace. The simple truth is that without his willingness to offer forgiveness and grace to us so freely, it would be inaccessible. The good news is that he does choose to offer it to us. We simply must realize our need for it, confess our sins, and accept it.

That process somehow seems complicated. Let's take the time to simplify it.

Realize our need for forgiveness.

Just as David missed the point of Nathan's story, so we often don't realize that we have sins that need forgiving. We run around in our own little world taking care of our own little business and never stop to consider the much larger picture of God and Satan, heaven and hell, sin and righteousness, right and wrong. God is always faithful even when we forget. He will send the Holy Spirit to remind us that we need him. He will send the Holy Spirit to declare to us, in the voice of the prophet Nathan, "You think that man is evil? You are that man." The preachers call it conviction—that deep, gnawing realization that we actually need to be forgiven for so many things in our lives. Mostly, we need to be forgiven for allowing everything else to take first place in our lives and leaving God with just the leftovers. We are proud of ourselves for giving him a few dollars a week and one hour of our time on Sunday. (As long as we don't have the chance to be out of town and the game isn't on.) We never confess our need for forgiveness because we never realize our need for forgiveness. We are so caught up in our excuses and rationalizations that we can't see the rotting carcass of our own integrity lying helplessly by the roadside. At least not until the prophet or the Holy Spirit shows up; he will point it out. He always does. That's his job.

Confess our need for forgiveness.

Then our prophet Nathan shows up, often in the person of the Holy Spirit. He speaks to us within our own hearts and condemns us from within. When our sins are brought to light, we are crushed by the reality of them. It is in that moment that we need to confess—not so much the particular sin (though we do need to confess that)—but the real problem. Listen to David's confession again: "I have sinned against the LORD" (2 Sam. 12:13). The real violation is against God. He is the one we reject when we choose to do things we know he doesn't want us to do. He is the one we reject when we choose to do things we know are wrong. He is the one we reject when we allow everything else to take first place over him. We need to confess our rejection of him. It is sin and it must be confessed, no matter what we think the consequences of that confession may be.

Surrender to our source of forgiveness.

I think it is interesting that Nathan consoles David by saying, "The LORD has taken away your sin. You are not going to die" (2 Sam. 12:13). I think David believed that he would be killed on the spot for his wrongdoing. Honestly, he deserved to be killed. He had committed murder. Under Jewish law, he had now committed numerous crimes that were punishable by death. So I think he believed his confession would be the last words out of his mouth.

We need to continue to remember the phrase I have repeated numerous times now: The consequences of confession always pale in comparison to the cost of concealment.

No matter what the consequences are going to be, we still need to confess our sins to our God. Then we trust in his grace to forgive us rather than fearing that his anger will kill us. If God was willing to forgive David for that laundry list of sins, the vast majority of us have literally nothing to fear. Listen to these words from Scripture: "Jesus Christ is the same yesterday and today and forever" (Heb. 13:8). And these words: "I the LORD do not change. So you, the descendants of Jacob, are not destroyed" (Mal. 3:6). The same God who chose to forgive David will choose to forgive you. Just realize your need for his forgiveness, confess the sins you have committed (understanding that they really are against him), and surrender to his forgiveness.

Here at New Life, we like to put it this way—remember your ABCs.

Admit that I have sinned against God and need a Savior.

For all have sinned and fall short of the glory of God.
—Romans 3:23

Believe that Jesus can and will forgive me, no matter what I have done.

If you declare with your mouth, "Jesus is Lord," and believe in your heart that God raised him from the dead, you will be saved.
—Romans 10:9

Commit to do the work of changing my ways to his ways, no matter what it costs.

Repent, then, and turn to God, so that your sins may be wiped out, that times of refreshing may come from the Lord.
—Acts 3:19

If you have never asked Jesus to be your Savior and forgive you of your sins, why not do it now?

24

A Heart That Is Broken

By doing this you have shown utter contempt for the LORD, the son born to you will die. After Nathan had gone home, the LORD struck the child that Uriah's wife had borne to David, and he became ill. David pleaded with God for the child. He fasted and spent the nights lying in sackcloth on the ground. The elders of his household stood beside him to get him up from the ground, but he refused, and he would not eat any food with them. On the seventh day the child died. David's attendants were afraid to tell him that the child was dead, for they thought, "While the child was still living, he wouldn't listen to us when we spoke to him. How can we now tell him the child is dead? He may do something desperate." David noticed that his attendants were whispering among themselves, and he realized the child was dead. "Is the child dead?" he asked. "Yes," they replied, "he is dead."

—2 Samuel 12:14–19

I don't mean to keep bringing this up, but . . .

Sin is *never* free.

Sin *always* kills.

The consequences of confession always pale in comparison to the cost of concealment.

David reaped the consequences of his sin, and it caused him tremendous grief. I need to dispel a myth here. Some people think—and, quite honestly, some preachers seem to say—that when one is forgiven, all sorrow is taken away. That just isn't true. The consequences of our sins can cause us great sorrow and grief for many years. Some sins, like this moment in David's life, will hurt for the rest of our lives. Forgiveness does not always relieve sorrow. It does, however, begin the process of healing.

David realized that his son was going to pay the price for his sin. He was devastated by what he had done. He began to plead with God for the child's life. I think the story would have a better ending if God had somehow miraculously healed the boy and allowed David to pay some other, more personal price, but that wasn't what God chose to do.

David did not give up.

He continued to believe in and trust a gracious God. He thought to himself, "Who knows? The LORD may be gracious to me and let the child live" (2 Sam. 12:22). So he kept praying, fasting, and begging God that his sin would not affect his son.

We can learn some things here.

On a negative note, we must realize that our sin can affect those we love the most. In fact, our sin will most likely affect those we love the most, because they are closer to us and therefore closer to our sin and our punishment. We must remember that our actions have consequences on the lives of other people. No choice I make is simply isolated to just me. A choice can cause pain to others or bring blessing to others. We must be extremely careful what we choose to do. It could have disastrous consequences, or it could bring amazing blessings. Ultimately, the choice is ours.

On a more positive note, we should never give up. God is gracious. Sometimes he will show kindness even when it isn't deserved. We should never stop praying for those we love the most. If God does not intervene in the way we want him to, he still hears our heart's cry. He understands our pain, feels our anguish, and sees our desires. He knows what we want, and he knows what is best. While we cannot always understand the choices he makes, we should never stop praying and pleading with him on behalf of those we love.

I have so many times begged God to protect those I love from the stupid things I may choose to do. I don't always have a particular stupid thing in mind when I pray. I just don't want those around me to be hurt by my actions, choices, or sins. So I follow the example I see here in David. I realize that my actions always have consequences, good or bad, and so I plead with God to protect those closest to me from the negative consequences of any choice I might make. Who knows? The Lord may be gracious to me.

25

A Heart That Needs to Be Sturdy

"Yes," they replied, "he is dead." Then David got up from the ground. After he had washed, put on lotions and changed his clothes, he went into the house of the LORD and worshiped. Then he went to his own house, and at his request they served him food, and he ate. His attendants asked him, "Why are you acting this way? While the child was alive, you fasted and wept, but now that the child is dead, you get up and eat." He answered, "While the child was still alive, I fasted and wept. I thought, 'Who knows? The LORD may be gracious to me and let the child live.' But now that he is dead, why should I go on fasting? Can I bring him back again? I will go to him, but he will not return to me." Then David comforted his wife Bathsheba, and he went to her and made love to her. She gave birth to a son, and they named him Solomon. The LORD loved him.
—2 Samuel 12:19–24

David's heart was back in the right place. You may remember this phrase: It is possible for a person to act, for a time, in a manner that is inconsistent with his heart, but it is impossible for a person to act, for a lifetime, in a manner that is inconsistent with his heart.

Now David was back to acting in a manner that was consistent with his heart. He realized what he had done wrong. He knew the punishment that had been weighed out. He accepted the responsibility of his actions and would live the rest of his life knowing what his actions did to his son. He realized even more than that. He knew he would see his son again some day. He knew that God had the boy in his arms and that he had already received his eternal reward.

So, David moved on.

I think this is where so many people get caught after a tragedy. They don't seem able to find a way to move on. They get stuck in a tragic, sad, devastated, lonely place, and they are just frozen there. Unable to move and unable to go back, they are just stuck. While I really am not qualified to offer real counsel here, let me suggest a simple process I think I see in David's reaction to this moment.

Step 1—Do what you know to do.

Once he realized the child was dead, the Bible says he "got up from the ground . . . washed, put on lotions and changed his clothes." In other words, he just did what was necessary at the moment. Honestly, in the devastating moments following a tragedy, just doing normal, everyday, mundane things can be a great victory. In fact, they can be healing and comforting. After all of that time fasting and weeping, David desperately needed to get cleaned up. He needed to get up off the ground and, at least externally, put himself together. For most of us, the first step of healing is just getting out of bed the day after a tragedy. It's not as easy as it sounds, but it is necessary.

Get up, clean up, and do what you know to do until you know what to do.

Somewhere along the way, you will begin to see flashes of hope, glimmers of joy, and streams of light that indicate a new day dawning. Until then, just keep doing the everyday, mundane things that keep life moving.

Step 2—Worship God.

This is often the last thing we want to do after a tragedy. Instead of worshiping him, we often want to blame him. In the absence of anyone else to blame, we lash out at the One who could have protected, healed, sheltered, or at least warned us—but didn't. So anger at God can set in, but that anger has no healing power.

Worship does.

When we worship God, we remind ourselves that we are not alone and powerless on this great, big, angry planet of ours. We remember that God is actually in control. We remember that he has promised us another life, and our loved ones will be there waiting for us when we get there. The God we want to be angry with is actually the only hope we have. Listen again to David's words: "But now that he is dead, why should I go on fasting? Can I bring him back again? I will go to him, but he will not return to me" (2 Sam. 12:23). Did you hear the hope in that? "I will go to him." The sorrow in knowing that "he will not return to me" is real. So is the hope that one day "I will go to him."

Step 3—Hold on to family.

Once David got himself together and worshiped God, he went to Bathsheba. He comforted her. In these moments, family is what we need to hold on to the tightest. They are, after all, going through the heartache of this tragedy with us. They need us to help them as much as we need them to help us. Family gets through tragedy together. If blood-related family is for some reason not an option, then those of the family of God who are journeying along with us on life's road are the ones we must hold tight. They will help us navigate these dark and frightening roads.

We need to always remember that God will ultimately heal all of us. I want to show you a couple things here.

God Will Change Our Status. When Nathan left David, the Bible says, "The LORD struck the child that Uriah's wife had borne to David" (2 Sam. 12:15). When David went to comfort Bathsheba, the Bible says, "David comforted his wife"

(2 Sam. 12:24). We have a real change in relationship here. When Bathsheba conceived the first child, she was Uriah's wife. Now she is David's wife. God is willing to bring healing even in the midst of our biggest sins.

God Gives a Future. "She gave birth to a son, and they named him Solomon. The LORD loved him" (2 Sam. 12:24). I have always found it interesting that the next king of Israel was the son of Bathsheba. This is a living testimony to God's grace. Solomon is proof that God does not punish us forever for sins we commit in a moment. He provides grace. He will even provide blessing. Solomon, the son of David, the son of Bathsheba, would serve mostly as a good king. God took what David messed up and used it to secure David's legacy and Bathsheba's future.

Praise his holy name!

PART 5

A FAITHFUL HEART

Godly hearts allow us to have courageous hearts. Those courageous hearts give us the confidence we need to develop hearts of grace. Hearts of grace will be important for us one day since we all have flawed hearts. Yet even with our flaws, we must learn to remain faithful. A faithful heart is not the most exciting thing we can pursue. Godliness, courage, and even flaws seem more exciting than faithfulness. Faithfulness is slow. It is mundane. It is boring.

I have often said that the world is changed through the consistent repetition of right things. Another way to say it is that we can change our world by being faithful in the mundane. While this is not exciting stuff, it is important stuff. God means for us to remain faithful, and failure to do so comes at a high price. In the following accounts from the life of David, we learn from his determined faithfulness, and we learn from his failure to show faithfulness. In that sense, David is a lot like us. So let us take look at the good and the bad, and learn from both.

26

Be Faithful to God's Commands

When you enter the land the LORD your God is giving you and have taken possession of it and settled in it, and you say, "Let us set a king over us like all the nations around us," be sure to appoint over you a king the LORD your God chooses. He must be from among your fellow Israelites. Do not place a foreigner over you, one who is not an Israelite. The king, moreover, must not acquire great numbers of horses for himself or make the people return to Egypt to get more of them, for the LORD has told you, "You are not to go back that way again." He must not take many wives, or his heart will be led astray. He must not accumulate large amounts of silver and gold.

—Deuteronomy 17:14–17

God, through Moses, gives us this passage in Scripture. It was written around 400 years prior to the anointing of King Saul. God knew the Israelites would eventually want a king. Prior to the arrival of King Saul, judges led the people, much in the pattern Moses set while he was alive and Joshua continued during his lifetime. A judge was clearly the one in charge, but there was no assumption of royalty and therefore no assumption of dynastic lines of father to son rulers. God knew that eventually his people would want to look more like the people of this world. So he set out some guidelines for the eventual king to follow:

God himself must choose the king through a prophet.

He must be a native Israelite.

He must not seek great military might for himself.

He must not have many wives.

He must not accumulate great wealth for himself.

Five commands don't seem all that complicated, but these rules literally only lasted through one king. As far as we can tell, King Saul kept all of these rules. Then he refused to give up power when God was done with him, and he lost his mind in the process of attempting to hold on to the throne. He is therefore not remembered as a good king. King David, on the other hand, violated a number of these. He was chosen by God and anointed by Samuel, the prophet. He was a native Israelite. But that's where the good news ends. David intentionally established himself as the most powerful military leader of his time. He and all of Israel grew very proud of their power. David had many wives, at least eight, and likely more. Some he married out of love, others out of political strategy, and others for various reasons. Again, his numerous wives became a source of pride for David and his kingdom. As for wealth, David had plenty. Estimates, adjusted to modern values, range from $1 billion to $8 billion. He was by far the wealthiest man of his day. Again, his wealth became a great source of pride for David and his kingdom.

With this in mind (and realizing that King David failed to follow three out of five of God's commands for a king), let's consider three things.

God gives commands for a reason.

When God gives a command, he does not do so to frustrate us or steal our fun. God's commands have purpose. In this case, God knew that any king who pursued the following would fail to stay focused on him.

- **Great military power.** A king who built a great army for himself could feel invincible and forget his need for God. In fact, God punished David later in life for counting his armies (see 2 Sam. 24). David likely had them counted so that he could take pride in how powerful he was. He repented before the Lord as soon as he did it, but it was too late to avoid punishment. In our daily lives, we may not be in the business of accumulating great armies that we can command into battles and wars, but we are in the business of amassing all of the authority and power we can find. When we allow that power, given to us by God, to overshadow our reliance on God, we fall into the same pride that God warned us about and King David suffered from in his later years.

- **Multiple wives.** This is a matter of pride. God wanted the pride of the king to be placed in the God who had anointed him in the first place, not in his own manliness. (The pursuit of manliness would be the modern equivalent of David having so many wives.) He had to prove what a great man he was, and he had to do that by having all of these wives and children. It was all part of the trappings of wealth and power. Today, this may not play out in multiple wives, but it could play out in multiple affairs—a trail of broken hearts and broken promises—all in the name of proving to be a great lover or great man.

- **Great wealth.** Even today, we see people becoming convinced that they do not need God because they have so much wealth. Too much wealth leaves us vulnerable to a type of pride that causes us to forget God and his faithfulness. Somehow we begin to believe that our wealth will give us the security and importance that really only comes from God. When we lose sight of our reliance on God due to our reliance on wealth, we run the risk of losing everything. Wealth comes and goes. Wealth really is a fickle thing; but God remains. Put your trust in what lasts.

What's in your safe? Better make sure it's a whole lot of reliance on God.

God gives grace even when commands are forgotten.

One of the most obvious takeaways we can discover here is that God is faithful to offer grace even when we are not faithful to follow his commands. There is always a price to be paid for failure to follow God's commands, but his grace is still always sufficient. There is no doubt that King David had read the commands in Deuteronomy, and yet the world around him demanded something different from a king. God wanted humility and simplicity in the life of the King of Israel. The world demanded that a king of David's stature be powerful, wealthy, have many wives, a huge army, and lots of gold. The world won. In the end, the wealth and power constantly challenged David's perspective. He constantly struggled against the strong current of pride, worldliness, greed, and arrogance. Only the fact that his heart, at its core, remained committed to God kept him humble enough to reach out to God for forgiveness and grace. When David reached out for God's forgiveness, God's grace was always there.

God's ways are always best.

God's ways really are the best ways. David built this great army without worrying about its size. God always provided the fighting force that David needed for whatever challenge he faced at the moment. David's reliance on God actually resulted in a fighting force of somewhere around 1.3 million men. That is impressive in today's terms and must have been terrifying to the enemies of Israel in David's day. David's reliance on

God brought him great wealth. His wealth is actually only able to be determined to a degree by looking at the gift he left behind for the building of the temple in Jerusalem. Again, it is God who provided all this wealth. As for the wives, I believe that actually caused a great deal of pain for David. (At least later in life, but we will deal with that later.) Just remember, and never forget, it was God's goodness that brought all this about, not David's brilliance.

And so it is with us. God gives us everything. All that we accomplish and all that we accumulate is from God. His goodness and grace provide what we need, and often a little more. He gives us the strength to work. He gives us the opportunity to advance. He gives us the wisdom to save. He gives us the talent to serve. He gives us everything we have or ever will have. We must be careful not to allow our blessings to become our curse. We can accomplish this by always remembering that our security and our value are not based on our accomplishments or our accumulation of wealth, but on the truth that we are created by, loved by, blessed by, and protected by the very hand of our creator God. We have value because he says so. That is better than money in the bank.

27

Be Faithful to My Family

In the course of time, Amnon son of David fell in love with Tamar, the beautiful sister of Absalom son of David [different mothers]. . . . But he [Amnon] refused to listen to her [Tamar], and since he was stronger than she, he raped her. Then Amnon hated her with intense hatred. In fact, he hated her more than he had loved her. . . . Absalom never said a word to Amnon, either good or bad; he hated Amnon because he had disgraced his sister Tamar. . . . Absalom ordered his men, "Listen. When Amnon is in high spirits from drinking wine and I say to you, 'Strike Amnon down,' then kill him. Don't be afraid. . . . So Absalom's men did to Amnon what Absalom had ordered. . . . Absalom fled and went to Geshur [where his grandfather on his mother's side was king], he stayed there three years. And King David longed to go to Absalom. . . . Then Joab went to Geshur and brought Absalom back to Jerusalem. But the king [David] said, "He must go to his own house; he must not see my face." So Absalom went to his own house and did not see the face of the king. . . . A messenger came and told David, "The hearts of the people of Israel are with Absalom." Then David said to all his officials who were with him in Jerusalem, "Come. We must flee. . . . Meanwhile,

*Absalom and all the men of Israel came to Jerusalem. . . .
So they pitched a tent for Absalom on the roof, and he
slept with his father's concubines in the sight of all Israel
[a sign of disgrace for King David and a show of power by
Absalom]. . . . And ten of Joab's armor-bearers surrounded
Absalom, struck him and killed him. . . . He [David] went
up to the room over the gateway and wept. As he went,
he said: "O my son Absalom. My son, my son Absalom.
If only I had died instead of you—O Absalom, my son, my
son." . . . Then King David said, "Call in Bathsheba." . . .
"As surely as the LORD lives, who has delivered me out
of every trouble, I will surely carry out this very day what
I swore to you by the LORD, the God of Israel: Solomon
your son shall be king after me. . . . But Adonijah [David's
son who is older than Solomon and expects to become
king], in fear of Solomon, went and took hold of the horns
of the altar [a cry for safety from one's enemies]. . . .
Now Adonijah, the son of Haggith, went to Bathsheba,
Solomon's mother. . . . "Please ask King Solomon—he will
not refuse you—to give me Abishag the Shunammite [King
David's final wife] as my wife." . . . Then King Solomon swore
by the LORD: "May God deal with me, be it ever so severely,
if Adonijah does not pay with his life for this request [the
request was actually a veiled play for the throne]. . . . So
King Solomon gave orders to Benaiah son of Jehoiada, and
he struck down Adonijah and he died.*

—portions from 2 Samuel 13:1—1 Kings 2:25

OK, let's be honest, this is one messed up family. Then again, what do you expect? Here we have a man with multiple wives, each of whom has kids, and all are, to one degree or another, related. (There must be some drama wrapped up in that somewhere.) David was so busy building wealth and power that he likely had very little time for any of them.

That is a recipe for a mess.

While it is true that most Americans don't face the challenges of polygamy today, we do face the challenges of working to build wealth and security while raising kids and maintaining a healthy relationship with our spouse. That can be a daunting task. Let me give you a simple set of thoughts that have helped me through the years.

Start with family.

My Grandpa Hilson was not always the easiest man. He was, at times, domineering and pushy. However, he did instill in me a deep appreciation for family. His father, my great-grandfather, was abandoned as a child and never knew his dad. His mother's family, the Campbells, raised Great-Grandpa Hilson. (This must have been very difficult for them since my great-grandfather was born as a result of an adulterous affair between his father and the Campbell's daughter-in-law. The man whose marriage was violated raised my great-grandfather. Though I have never met them, the Campbells must be wonderful people.) My great-grandfather and great-grandmother died in a flu outbreak when Grandpa Hilson was younger than ten years old. So

Grandpa Hilson went back to Alabama and he, too, was raised by the very same Campbell family. These events left Grandpa Hilson with a deep longing for an established family. He talked about it all the time. He was constantly trying to find out where we came from, and that was difficult work in the days before the internet. So he instilled in me a desire for an established, strong, multigenerational family unit before I was even married. I started my marriage with that as an established goal.

Stay with family.

This is not as easy as it sounds. My dad didn't have my same goal of family life stability. He spent many years chasing after happiness and fulfillment in less than godly ways. (Today my dad is an ordained minister once again and is serving the Lord effectively in his retirement years. Praise the Lord for his faithfulness.) To my Grandpa Hilson's heartbreak, my sister and I were raised by our stepdad, Gray Goodman. Now the Goodmans were raising the Hilsons, which worked out. The Goodmans, my family, lived on Bradshaw Road, and my stepdad's mom was a Bradshaw. If you want to see multigenerational stability, you need look no further than the Bradshaws. They had lived on and worked the land for many generations, and many of them still live nearby to this day. What is the difference between my dad and my stepdad? Both are really good men. Both are wise and dedicated in their own ways and to their own goals. The only real difference, at least the only difference that mattered to me, was that my stepdad stayed. Honestly, this is one of the great, unromantic secrets to stability: just don't leave. Figure out what's wrong, fix what's broken, work on what you have to, and stay home. I learned that from my mom, my grandparents, both Hilsons and Freemans, and the Goodmans-Bradshaws.

End with family.

So here we are. Our kids are grown, and Tina and I are still together and going strong. We may still feel like we are in our twenties (and sometimes we act like it), but we aren't. I must say that Grandpa Hilson would be thrilled. Three sons. Stable marriage. Hope for the future of the Hilson name.

I intend to keep it that way.

The day will come when I will lie in some bed and gasp for my final breaths. I have already determined that I will walk now in such a way that I will not be alone then. By keeping my family first and staying to the end, even when the demands of life interfere, I trust that God will allow me to see my kids, my grandkids, and even my great-grandkids living together in the love, peace, and stability that Tina and I have been determined to provide. Truth is, family isn't easy. It isn't quick. Family doesn't happen overnight, and family is not established just because you make babies. Family takes work, but it is always worth it.

That kind of family life has, so far, served me well.

That kind of family life would have served David and the nation of Israel well.

That kind of family life would serve you well, too.

So do the work and choose today that you will stay even when it gets tough. Then trust God to build peace and stability into the family for which you are giving your life.

28

Be Faithful to God's Desire for Peace

And Absalom never said a word to Amnon, either good or bad; he hated Amnon because he had disgraced his sister Tamar.

—2 Samuel 13:22

Amnon, son of David, had raped his half sister, Tamar, whose full brother was Absalom. As far as we can tell, King David did nothing to punish Amnon for his behavior. The Bible says that King David "was furious" when he heard about it (see 2 Sam. 13:21). The Bible does not give us any indication that anything was done to bring justice for Tamar.

Absalom was filled with rage.

God desires peace in our world and in our families. Many people have a wrong understanding of peace. They may see it as a lack of arguing or fighting. Therefore, in order to accomplish this kind of peace, they simply overlook problems and sweep conflict under the rug. However, that will not work. Ignoring problems and overlooking violations does not attain peace. Peace is difficult work and must be constantly pursued. By looking at what David failed to do, we will learn how to handle sticky and potentially explosive conflicts. Let me suggest three action items I think David should have put into place but did not. While this work will be uncomfortable and difficult, remember that the cost of failure, in this case, was that Absalom's rage brought death into David's family, divided the kingdom of Israel, and brought shame to an entire nation.

Conflict must be dealt with or it will be deadly.

In order to achieve restoration and peace when a wrong has taken place within your family, among your friends, at your workplace, church, or any relationship group, take these three steps:

- **Deal with it quickly.** Absalom felt that it was his responsibility to defend the honor of his sister, because David did not do anything to punish Amnon for his actions. Honestly, I have always wondered what would have happened in the story if David had punished Amnon properly. With justice served, would Absalom have lived out the rest of his days peacefully? This is an important question because, with the exception of Solomon (who would be the next king), Absalom appears to have been the most driven and talented leader among David's sons. Could he have turned out to be a great king? Could he have turned out to be a great leader alongside his brother Solomon? Could this story have been dramatically different had David done the right thing instead of the easy thing? We will never know. What we do know is that David's failure to do anything sent Absalom to the darkest of places and ultimately drove him to kill his half-brother, Amnon. David's failure to deal with the issues in his family had already turned deadly and, sadly, it wasn't over.

Absalom ran to his mother's father and David's father-in-law, Talmai King of Geshur. He hid there for three years. Though the Bible clearly tells us that "David longed to go to Absalom," there is no indication that he actually ever made contact (see 2 Sam. 13:39). No effort to see his son. No attempts made to rebuke, train, console, or direct him. No contact whatsoever. No resolution from David after the rape of his sister, Tamar. No contact from David after the murder of Amnon. No response from a father who obviously needed to deal with his wayward son. So Absalom just stewed.

This is what happens when you don't deal with conflict quickly. People just stew in the anger and bitterness of the inaction, especially if you are in a position of authority or power. People expect action when conflict is tearing at the fabric of your people. Whether real or simply perceived, the silence of a person in authority, a parent, boss, neighbor, or friend is interpreted as a lack of concern. This can add to the fires of hatred, hurt, and resentment.

- **Deal with it personally.** After three years of silence from his father, Absalom received a visit from Joab, the commander of David's army. Joab had finally convinced King David to allow him to bring Absalom back to Jerusalem. Here was the problem: David should have gone to get Absalom himself. He was Absalom's father. He was the one who "longed to go to Absalom." He was the one who had failed to deal with Amnon, and it was Amnon's arrogance, lust, and lack of self-control that had started this whole mess. Yet it wasn't David who went to Absalom to ask him to come home, it was one of David's employees. Honestly, that was really insulting.

  When you send someone else to deal with something that you should be dealing with personally, you communicate, at the very least, a lack of concern, and, at the worst, arrogance or dismissiveness. It says: "This problem and this person are beneath me. They really don't matter." That is likely how Absalom felt when it was Joab who brought him back. I imagine him saying, "Wow, I'm not important enough to my dad for him to come get me himself!" That is not a good starting point for reconciliation. No matter how difficult or painful it's going to be, if the problem is yours to fix, do it quickly and do it personally. No one else can fix your mess. It takes your insight, your touch, your repentance, your time, and your effort. If you are expecting someone else to go and bring a solution to the troubles you have caused or allowed to exist, you are going to be disappointed.

- **Deal with it completely.** Then David did it again. After Joab brought Absalom back to Jerusalem, David wouldn't meet with him. It took two more years and a meeting arranged through Joab before Absalom was allowed to even see his father. Let me be honest. If you are not willing to see reconciliation through to the end, then don't even start. At first, we had an angry child whose father was not responding to a very real hurt (Amnon raped his sister). Then an angry, murderous child fled to another country to find refuge from a father who was so distant that the child didn't even know if his father wanted to kill him. Then the angry child was brought back into the city, but his father would not talk to him. Why would anyone do that? Oh, I know; let's bring the angry one home and ignore him. That will make it better. It makes no sense at all. It set up the coup that would almost destroy David's kingdom.

When you start working toward reconciliation, see it through. If you don't, you communicate very negative things to your children, your coworkers, your employees, your neighbors, your . . . whomever. If David had quickly dealt with Amnon's sin, personally dealt with Absalom's anger, or even just completely cleared the table with Absalom once he was back home, then maybe this story could have ended differently.

He didn't.

You can.

Be serious about peace, especially in your family. Deal with conflict quickly, personally, and completely, and then trust the Holy Spirit to bring peace.

In wrapping up this thought, let me give you a perspective that has helped me through the years. There is a dramatic difference between a peacekeeper and a peacemaker.

Peacekeepers

A peacekeeper is a horrible role to play. They resolve nothing. They help nothing. In the end, they accomplish nothing. They are not there to solve problems or actually bring healing or resolution to conflict. They are simply there to jump between two angry parties whenever the inevitable fight breaks out. Often the peacekeeper is the one who gets bloodied.

I remember as a young man watching United Nations peacekeepers at work in some war-torn part of the world. I was shocked as I watched the news reporter tell the story of these well-meaning, brave men and women. These people were in a war zone, and in that particular situation, they were not given any weapons. They were dressed in these soft-looking, baby blue helmets, unarmed, and wandering the streets of a war zone. I couldn't tell you the year or what the conflict was, because I was pretty young at the time, but the image of snipers taking them down one at a time has never left me.

Peacekeepers are little more than targets. It is a thankless and ineffective job. I resolved that if I had any choice at all, I would never be a peacekeeper.

Peacemakers

A peacemaker is different. They are there to fix something. Status quo is not the end goal of a peacemaker. The peacemaker is not there to break up the fight. They find the problem that caused the fight. They are armed, they do not wear some soft, baby blue hat, and they are not there to be targets. They are to be respected and even feared. A peacemaker will not only allow conflict in certain situations, but will enter the conflict and fight alongside the parties, if that fight will help bring about resolution. Sometimes resolution requires a fight.

King David made the unfortunate choice to be a peacekeeper among his children. He attempted to sweep Amnon's rape of Tamar under the rug and hide it. He attempted to ignore Absalom's rage and hope it would just go away. He attempted to solve a problem by acting like the problem never existed. As a result, he became little more than a target. Had he chosen instead to be a peacemaker, he would have jumped in at the very moment that Amnon committed such a heinous act and fought alongside Absalom for the honor of Absalom's sister (and his daughter). At that point, this situation could have ended very differently. Take a lesson from the failure of David, and remember that God desires and honors unity. God desires and honors peacemaking. God blesses those who deal with conflict quickly and properly.

God is no peacekeeper.

God is a peacemaker.

Isn't that exactly what Jesus did on the cross? He took on the source of our problem: sin. He defeated it. He fought. He won. Therefore, we are free.

So, I guess what I'm saying is that you shouldn't be afraid to fight for what will bring healing and understanding. When you fight, fight for the right things.

Don't fight in anger; fight in love.

David's love for Tamar should have motivated him to fight alongside Absalom for the righteousness and integrity of his family.

Don't fight to win; fight to understand.

Absalom, in his rage, fought only to win. Only to destroy those with whom he was angry. In the end, he never came to understand the love that his father actually had for him.

Don't fight like a jerk; fight like a friend.

Friends fight. Sometimes those fights are intense, and to the rest of the world, they may seem angry and brutal. When true friends fight, they never end up angry. They fight, then they reach an understanding, then they laugh. I have always preferred people around me who are willing to fight with me. Even though the fights can be intense, at least I never wonder what they are really thinking. I would rather my friends hurt my feelings in an attempt to help than lie to me in an attempt to hide.

Fight for what is right and against what is wrong.

Keep in mind that when we, in an attempt to be peace-keepers, cover over injustice or sin, we actually endorse the sin that caused the conflict in the first place. We normalize what is wrong, to the detriment of what is right. We end up on the wrong side of the argument, the wrong side of the conflict, and the wrong side of history.

29

Be Faithful to My Role

> *A messenger came and told David, "The hearts of the people of Israel are with Absalom." Then David said to all his officials who were with him in Jerusalem, "Come. We must flee, or none of us will escape from Absalom. We must leave immediately, or he will move quickly to overtake us and bring ruin on us and put the city to the sword." The king's officials answered him, "Your servants are ready to do whatever our lord the king chooses."*
> —2 Samuel 15:13–15

Commentators disagree on David's options here. Some say that David was sitting in the most fortified city and therefore the most fortified palace in the world. His retreat out of the city was an unnecessary show of failure and lack of faith in his men and his God. This scenario is entirely plausible. As I think through it, it seems true to me that David was convinced that this onslaught from Absalom was entirely his fault and that he would therefore do nothing to rise up against his son. So David was willing to let the city and ultimately the nation fall, because he was unwilling to deal with the past demons of his own family. In other words, it was an unnecessary retreat based on David's guilt, not on the inability of Israel's army to protect the king and city.

Others say we can't assume that David had any supporting army left. They claim that Absalom had completely won over the hearts of David's men, that there may only have been a handful left with David, and that they would stand no chance against the full onslaught of the rest of Israel's fighting force. These folks would argue that David was doing the right thing by getting out of town so that he could regroup and stage a counterattack.

I'm really not sure which one is right. I tend to think that David gave up. I think he had no stomach for a fight with Absalom and knew he could never harm his son. You just can't win a fight against someone you are not willing to hurt. He did not want to see Absalom killed by his supporters, but he knew that if he stayed and fought, they would kill his son. So, he chose to run. Don't make the mistake of thinking it was his only choice. Listen to the response of his officials again: "The king's officials answered him, 'Your servants are ready to do whatever our lord the king chooses'" (2 Sam. 15:15). These men were ready to fight. They were ready for whatever David chose.

David chose to run.

Quite honestly, this is not the first time David ran away from his problems. It was the first time he had run away from a fight, but not from his problems. David had been running away from Absalom for at least five years. He had ignored, hid, or run from the problems with his kids all along. Now it was coming back to bite him, and the entire nation was going to pay the price for his failure. His failure to lead, to punish, to comfort, and to play the role he had always played—came at an unimaginably high cost.

Faithful in My Role as Parent

There are at least two roles David should have been faithful to in his life. The first is the role of dad. Had he remained faithful in this role, it is reasonable to believe that none of this family conflict would have happened. Perhaps had he been a more faithful father, Amnon would not have raped Tamar. Certainly, had he dealt properly with Amnon, Absalom would not have developed such a hatred for David and the rest of his family. Had he properly dealt with Absalom after the murder of Amnon, he likely could have brought peace back to his household and to his nation. Had he dealt properly with Absalom after he returned to Israel—well, you get the point.

For those of us who are parents, the responsibility to properly play our God-given roles in the lives of our children and within the context of our families is imperative. I just can't emphasize enough the importance of proper parenting. While there is no guarantee that a child will follow the lead of a good parent, it certainly does help the odds. God has called us to handle our families and children properly. We cannot abdicate that responsibility to anyone for any reason. While it may be true that we must use childcare while we are working, the hours spent with our children must be savored for all they are worth. As parents, we must parent. If we refuse to do so, we are setting our children up for lives filled with hurt, rejection, anger, and pain.

One of the most common indicators and causes of poverty in any culture is the breakdown of the family unit. When there is only one parent present in the life of a child, that child suffers. When there are no parents present, the child faces nearly insurmountable odds. I don't mean to sound overly dramatic here, but I do believe this to be true. Parenting is the answer to societal poverty. Even when poverty exists, an intact family unit allows the parents and children to find joy and meaning in facing the adversity together. Failing to remain faithful to our role as parents is destructive in every aspect of our children's lives and our society at large.

If you are a parent, then let me be blunt:

Get over yourself.

Be a parent.

Faithful in My Role as Leader

David also had a role to play as king, and he was going to let that one slide, too. Whether the odds were for or against him really shouldn't have mattered. David should have stayed and defended his city. The David of a few years ago would not have turned to run. You might think, "Well, if he fights,

Absalom will get killed. He has to protect Absalom." If that is what you're thinking, then you are likely thinking the exact same thing David was thinking. However, I'm going to ask you to look a little deeper. Yes, Absalom was David's son. No, David did not want Absalom hurt or killed. Absalom also was an angry, unstable young man. What kind of future would Jerusalem or Israel have had under that kind of leadership? Death and pain were going to follow Absalom because they were all he knew. By the time Absalom began working on his rebellion plan, it was too late. Death was the only possible end for him. If it didn't come at the hand of David and his army, it would come at the hand of someone who rose up later to overthrow what would certainly have been an evil and vindictive King Absalom.

David likely knew this.

I think that David experienced a deep depression at this time. He knew that he had failed and didn't know how to fix it. He wasn't willing to kill Absalom, and yet he knew that was likely the only solution. So rather than stand and face the challenge, a broken and depressed king turned to run, leaving a city and a nation in the hands of a murderous traitor.

Unfortunately, that kind of ending was all too predictable. When parents reject their God-given roles as parents, children suffer. When leaders reject their God-given roles as leaders, organizations and people suffer. When kings and presidents reject their God-given roles as leaders, nations suffer. We must be faithful to the roles God gives us, even when faithfulness is filled with painfulness. Jesus gives us a warning in Luke 12:48: "From everyone who has been given much, much will be demanded; and from the one who has been entrusted with much, much more will be asked." This warning must be heeded. God expects our faithfulness in the roles in which we are placed. He demands it. Our failure to remain faithful will have consequences far beyond our own banishment or even our own deaths. The scars left behind by unfaithful leaders and unfaithful parents take generations to heal. It is best to remain faithful now and avoid the negative patterns altogether.

30

Be Faithful to My Calling

Joab was told, "The king is weeping and mourning for Absalom." And for the whole army the victory that day was turned into mourning, because on that day the troops heard it said, "The king is grieving for his son." The men stole into the city that day as men steal in who are ashamed when they flee from battle. The king covered his face and cried aloud, "O my son Absalom. O Absalom, my son, my son." Then Joab went into the house to the king and said, "Today you have humiliated all your men, who have just saved your life and the lives of your sons and daughters and the lives of your wives and concubines. You love those who hate you and hate those who love you. You have made it clear today that the commanders and their men mean nothing to you. I see that you would be pleased if Absalom were alive today and all of us were dead. Now go out and encourage your men. I swear by the LORD that if you don't go out, not a man will be left with you by nightfall. This will be worse for you than all the calamities that have come on you from your youth till now." So the king got up and took his seat in the gateway. When the men were told, "The king is sitting in the gateway," they all came before him.

—2 Samuel 19:1–8

I suppose there are few things more difficult than going out to lead when all you want to do is curl up in a corner and die. That is the choice that was facing David. We all face, or will face, moments when there is just no fight left in us. We honestly would just as soon spend our days sleeping, crying, or hiding. We have no desire to see anyone and absolutely no desire to lead anyone. But leading and serving is our job. Leading and serving is our calling.

Whether you are a parent leading children, a pastor leading a church, a business owner leading employees, a commander leading the military, or an elected official leading a community, it is a calling that God has placed on you, a responsibility God has given you. You must follow through with it no matter how dark things may seem around you. Those people you are leading didn't cause your pain, and even if they did, they still need direction and encouragement from you. It's your responsibility. They need you.

How? How do you lead others forward when you don't know where to go or what to do? How can you lead others when your own pain, guilt, and tears blind you?

How?

Two suggestions.

Listen to your Joab.

You gotta give it to Joab. David's general was standing up for his king, and during this really dark period in David's life, it was Joab who had all the answers. Joab was the one who forced David to try and deal with Absalom after the murder of Amnon. It was Joab who finally ordered the death of Absalom so that the war could end and peace could resume. It was Joab who intervened with the king before the entire nation abandoned this depressed king who would trade them all in just to get his angry, broken, murderous son back.

Fortunately, I am convinced that God always sends us a Joab: someone who looks into our lives and sees what we don't see, who can make sense of the dark moments that seem to blind us. When we are blinded by tears, the Joabs in our lives take us by the hand, or kick us in the butt, and lead us through. So let me encourage you to find your Joab. He or she likely is already there; perhaps you just haven't recognized him yet or noticed what he is doing. Find him, and when you do, follow Joab until the king (I'm talking about you) thinks clearly again.

Straighten your back.

I once heard the story of a preacher who was caught in a moment when he just simply lacked the faith to lead on. As he sat devastated and confused, he confessed his lack of faith to a friend (who happened to be his Joab). The friend's response was pure gold: "Until you find your faith, borrow mine." You see, the more responsibility you have as a leader, the less space you have for lack of faith and direction. The more people look to you for direction, encouragement, hope, and courage, the less you have the luxury of collapse and surrender. You have to lead. They need you to lead, even if you can't figure out how.

It seems impossible.

When you have a Joab who is willing to loan you his faith until you regain your own, you can do the impossible. You can take the borrowed faith of a friend, straighten up your back, stand strong, and lead. You might have to "fake it 'till you make it," but in the end, you're not really faking anything. You are standing in the very real faith of another.

God will bless this.

I remember times when I just didn't feel like being the pastor. Now don't get me wrong: I love my job, and I live for the calling God has placed on my life. However, there are days when I am just not feeling it. On these days, someone always comes along and loans me some faith. My wife, someone on our leadership team, another pastor, a friend, even my mom, have loaned me faith in moments when I thought I just couldn't do it. When I take that little bit of borrowed faith and straighten my back and move on, an amazing thing happens: God shows up. By the time I find myself in the heat of the moment leading, speaking, writing, thinking, or whatever, God has changed my perspective and I can hand back the borrowed faith, because I have enough of my own.

So listen, I know the darkness inside of you gets really dark sometimes. Until you have enough faith to make it on your own, borrow some of mine. I am convinced that God has better days ahead for you.

31

Be Faithful to My Friends

On that day Gad [the Prophet of God] went to David and said to him, "Go up and build an altar to the Lord on the threshing floor of Araunah the Jebusite." So David went up, as the Lord had commanded through Gad. When Araunah looked and saw the king and his officials coming toward him, he went out and bowed down before the king with his face to the ground. Araunah said, "Why has my lord the king come to his servant?" "To buy your threshing floor," David answered, "so I can build an altar to the Lord, that the plague on the people may be stopped." Araunah said to David, "Let my lord the king take whatever he wishes and offer it up. Here are oxen for the burnt offering, and here are threshing sledges and ox yokes for the wood. Your Majesty, Araunah gives all this to the king." Araunah also said to him, "May the Lord your God accept you." But the king replied to Araunah, "No, I insist on paying you for it. I will not sacrifice to the Lord my God burnt offerings that cost me nothing." So David bought the threshing floor and the oxen and paid fifty shekels of silver for them. David built an altar to the Lord there and sacrificed burnt offerings and fellowship offerings. Then the Lord answered his prayer in behalf of the land, and the plague on Israel was stopped.
—2 Samuel 24:18–25

David had caused God to react in anger. David had decided to count all of the men in his army, and as we have already discussed, this was likely out of some sense of personal pride or arrogance that God could not overlook. So God set out punishment on Israel for the sin of David.

Let me clear something up here that I think could be bothering you, since it used to bother me. Why is it that so many Israelites died so that David could be punished? They didn't call for the count. It just doesn't seem fair, does it? David was even perplexed by this:

When David saw the angel who was striking down the people, he said to the LORD, "I have sinned; I, the shepherd, have done wrong. These are but sheep. What have they done? Let your hand fall on me and my family."

—2 Samuel 24:17

The truth is, it's not fair—but it did happen.

When national or international leaders make mistakes, the result is often the death of some of those who follow them, count on them, voted for them, or fought for them. This is a sad but true reality. I have often said I would never want to be president of the United States of America. Can you imagine? Every day that person must make decisions that will bring life or death to someone. Every choice the president makes is life altering. There are no small matters in the Oval Office. And so it was with King David. His choice cost many Israelites their lives, and he had to put a stop to it.

That is where we pick up this account. In an attempt to stop the plague he had caused, David was going to build an altar on a particular spot and offer sacrifices, as he had been instructed to do by the prophet Gad. A man named Araunah, who was a good man, owned the place where the altar was to go. He saw the suffering of his neighbors and was willing to play any role he could to bring a stop to it. He even offered to simply give the king all the land and cattle necessary for the offering to be made. Araunah was willing to sacrifice for his neighbors and his family. Like I said, he was a good man.

David refused to take the items for free. He insisted on paying for them. In doing this, I think we learn some very valuable lessons in how to handle our friendships and relationships in times of crisis.

Pay your own debts.

Don't let someone else pay the price of your sin. This calamity was David's fault. Araunah was willing to cover the entire cost of fixing it, and no one would have faulted David for taking him up on the offer. After all, if Araunah wanted to contribute, who was David to steal his blessing? David knew there was a deeper issue. This debt was David's to pay, not Araunah's. David was the one who needed to pay the price of making it right. So, practically put, thank God for the generosity of the Araunahs in our lives, but stand up and pay your own debts. It's OK to accept help once in a while, but be careful about letting someone else pay the price of your mistakes. When you do that, you open up the potential of falling into a victim's mind-set. Once you are convinced that you are a victim, you will remain one until someone helps shift your perspective back to the victor you are in Christ.

Be a blessing, not a burden.

This leads directly to my next warning. Don't take advantage of a friend's generosity. Again, no one would have given it a second thought had David taken Araunah up on his generous offer. They would have praised Araunah's kindness and would have never questioned David's motive. However, Araunah would always know that the king, who was by far wealthier than he was, took advantage of a moment and allowed Araunah, who did nothing wrong, to pay the price that the king owed. David could not let that happen.

I honestly wish that, even in the church, we understood this kind of thinking. I wish that we were all a bit more careful about allowing someone else to pay for our mistakes. Quite honestly, in today's American culture, there is almost an expectation that someone else should pay for our poor choices. We've seen this play out in so many situations through the years. We all seem to expect the government to bail us out whenever we get into trouble, and sometimes our government is the cause of our troubles. Our leaders sometimes make choices that bring great pain to the people they are supposed to protect. Then everyone starts to point fingers at others, demanding that someone else bail them out. When, all the while, the healthiest answer is that we bail ourselves out. Sure there are moments when we must have the help of a friend, a neighbor, a family member, or the government. Just don't become dependent on that help. If you do, you are no longer yours. Generosity, offered with strings, is little more than enslavement.

Years ago, I sat in a foreign country with a friend from that country. He began to describe for me an opportunity he was excited about that would allow him to move to the United States. He had found a "friend" who was willing to give him a house, a vehicle, and a job if he would come to the US and work for him. Now, this young man was not really needy in his home country. He was well trained and had a good job. He had already begun building a house for his young family, paying with cash as he went. It gave me great pain to have to implore him to stay away from the United States. When he asked me why I thought the job wasn't a good idea, I told him: "If this friend owns the house you live in, the car you drive, the company you work for, and brings you into the US without proper documentation, he will own you." Once I began to describe these concerns, my young friend decided to stay home. Thank God.

When we allow others to pay our debts and carry our weight, we lose our sense of independence. We lose something of our self-worth. We lose our pride. In the end, whether intentional or not, we will lose our freedom.

I've been pretty hard on David recently. We have spent a lot of time dealing with some of his worst moments. But here he got it right. This disaster was his fault, so the cost of fixing it was coming out of his account.

David chose to say: "Hey Araunah, thanks, man. You are awesome and I really appreciate your kindness. I caused this, so I'm gonna clean it up. In fact, let me pay you a little extra for your trouble. God bless."

32

Be Faithful to My God

Have mercy on me, my God, have mercy on me, for in you I take refuge. I will take refuge in the shadow of your wings until the disaster has passed. I cry out to God Most High, to God, who vindicates me. He sends from heaven and saves me, rebuking those who hotly pursue me—God sends forth his love and his faithfulness. I am in the midst of lions; I am forced to dwell among ravenous beasts—men whose teeth are spears and arrows, whose tongues are sharp swords. Be exalted, O God, above the heavens; let your glory be over all the earth. They spread a net for my feet—I was bowed down in distress. They dug a pit in my path—but they have fallen into it themselves. My heart, O God, is steadfast, my heart is steadfast; I will sing and make music. Awake, my soul. Awake, harp and lyre. I will awaken the dawn. I will praise you, Lord, among the nations; I will sing of you among the peoples. For great is your love, reaching to the heavens; your faithfulness reaches to the skies. Be exalted, O God, above the heavens; let your glory be over all the earth.

—Psalm 57

David wrote this psalm, or song, as he was running for his life from King Saul. At the beginning of Psalm 57, the notation says that it was written "when he had fled from Saul into the cave." It's actually pretty incredible that while living in damp, dark caves, David was able to write such a beautiful song of praise, trust, and surrender. There is no doubt that David was grateful to God for his faithfulness and glory. Let me show you a few things I pick up from this story that can help us to remain faithful to the God who has always been faithful to us.

God's mercy is available, if I ask.

David began this song with the words, "Have mercy on me, my God, have mercy on me, for in you I take refuge" (Ps. 57:1). God's mercy is boundless. He will intervene on our behalf more times than we can count. Truth is, we all will face moments in the back of some cave that we didn't ask for or deserve—the dark moments when we realize that unless God intervenes, we aren't going to make it. David was facing such a moment. A young leader with a small band of fierce fighters was really no match for the entire army of Israel. King Saul had pointed that army directly at David and his men. They were reduced to hiding. In the back of some cave, the future king, the man who would soon be the wealthiest and most powerful man on the planet, crouched and hid.

God's mercy is always clearly visible in caves. It's obviously what we need, completely what we want, and truly the only way we are going to make it.

The enemies are real, but they are already defeated.

"They dug a pit in my path—but they have fallen into it themselves" (Ps. 57:6). God had already anointed David to be the next king. Saul may have still held the throne, but he was already done. God's plan would prevail. David knew this. Notice how he reacted to that knowledge. There was no falsely placed arrogance that drove him out of the cave to go toe-to-toe with King Saul. There was only submission to the God who had a timetable and was going to put David on that throne in his time. Saul was a real enemy. Saul was a dangerous enemy. David realized that in God's economy, Saul was a defeated enemy.

When we are walking in God's will, we need not to fear any enemy.

God is always more.

"Be exalted, O God, above the heavens; let your glory be over all the earth" (Ps. 57:11). As I write this, I have run off to a family member's house on a North Carolina beach to escape all distractions. Earlier, as I took my morning walk to set my head for the day of writing, I looked out and saw a group of surfers waiting for that perfect wave. Now, the coast of North Carolina is not known as a great place to surf, but for some reason the waves have been really good this week. As I watched the surfers, I thought about what they were doing. They were floating on top of the ocean, waiting for a wave, and they had absolutely no idea when it was going to show up.

That struck a chord with me. Just like those surfers, we find ourselves on the surface of God's will, creation, and power. We float there and wait. We wait for a wave of his energy to draw us up and propel us forward. As we float, we realize that we are so tiny on top of this massive presence. Like a single surfer on the surface of the ocean, we are little more than a speck on the face of his will. And we wait. We are honestly not even very safe. Here on top of this massive presence, we are not even at the top of the food chain. Contrary to popular opinion, God is not safe. He is massive. He is powerful. He is all-encompassing.

He is wild.

God is wild in the sense that we don't understand him. Wild in the sense that we have no idea what he is going to do next. Wild in the sense that we have no right to question or no power to change his hand, his movement, and his will. And we wait, oddly peaceful, strangely fulfilled, on the surface of this wild, dangerous, all-encompassing, all-powerful yet kind and somehow gentle God.

Then it happens. He sends the wave. That burst of energy that lifts us up and allows us to stand for the first time in what seems like forever. We feel strength, power, thrill, adrenaline, and respect as we tenderly rise to our feet with the power of the Almighty underneath us. This is our moment. The moment we had been waiting for, the moment we had hoped God would provide. This is it.

We have no control over the arrival of the wave.

We do have control over how skillfully we ride it.

Let me make a suggestion. Whatever it takes, whatever it costs, wait. Wait for that unknowable moment when the power of God lifts you up—then ride, and ride well.

PART 6

A WORSHIPING HEART

God is the one who gives us our hearts. He gives us the capacity for a godly heart. It is only in him that we can ever find a courageous heart. His forgiveness offered so freely to us is our model of a heart of grace. He is the only hope for our flawed hearts. It is to him and his ways that we commit our hearts. God is our everything.

King David seemed to understand this better than anyone. He may have had all of the trappings of a great life and success. He may have been handsome, smart, strong, brave, well trained, and truly loved. In the end, he always remembered that without God, he was nothing.

God is everything.

When we realize that God is everything, we realize that we simply must worship him. Jesus is really poignant on this issue. When confronted by the Pharisees, a religious group that hated him, Jesus said to them: "If they keep quiet, the stones will cry out" (Luke 19:40). God will be praised. All of creation yearns for the opportunity to cry out praises to the God of heaven. When we truly realize who he is, we too will yearn for and seek out every opportunity to lift up his glorious name. Praise God!

33

Worshiping in God's Spirit

David again brought together all the able young men of Israel—thirty thousand. He and all his men went to Baalah in Judah to bring up from there the ark of God, which is called by the Name, the name of the LORD Almighty, who is enthroned between the cherubim on the ark. They set the ark of God on a new cart and brought it from the house of Abinadab, which was on the hill. Uzzah and Ahio, sons of Abinadab, were guiding the new cart with the ark of God on it, and Ahio was walking in front of it. David and all Israel were celebrating with all their might before the LORD, with castanets, harps, lyres, timbrels, sistrums and cymbals.
—2 Samuel 6:1–5

To wrap this up, let's talk about worship and the presence of God in our lives. In 1 Samuel 6 and in 1 Chronicles 13, we get a dual description of David bringing the ark of the covenant (ark of God or ark of the Lord) to the capital city of Jerusalem, or the city of David. This is the same ark that was built by Moses and placed in the tabernacle. It represented the very presence of God among his people, Israel. When the ark was in the tabernacle as the people were encamped while wandering in the desert during the life of Moses, the presence of God hovered over the stationary ark in the form of a pillar of fire by night or a pillar of cloud by day. When the pillar of cloud or fire moved, the people packed up and moved with it.

In all the travels of the Israelites, whenever the cloud lifted from above the tabernacle, they would set out; but if the cloud did not lift, they did not set out—until the day it lifted. So the cloud of the Lord was over the Tabernacle by day, and fire was in the cloud by night, in the sight of all the Israelites during all their travels.

—Exodus 40:36–38

So as you can imagine, the arrival of the ark of the Lord in Jerusalem, the new capital of Israel, was a significant cause for excitement and celebration. It meant that the spirit of God was with them.

Let's consider a few things we need to understand about the presence of God in our lives today.

Living without the presence of God is crazy.

"Let us bring the ark of our God back to us, for we did not inquire of it during the reign of Saul" (1 Chron. 13:3). What?

King Saul "did not inquire" of the spirit of God during his reign? No wonder he failed. No wonder he found it impossible to remain true. No wonder he became insecure. No wonder he lost his mind.

When Tina and I were in college, I would go home over the summers and work for her dad in his upholstery shop. I remember being in the shop on a particularly difficult day. I don't remember the problem; I just remember that there were problems. Her dad looked at me and said, "I just don't know what people who don't believe in God do with days like this one." True. Without the presence of God in our lives, how are we to find direction, insight, wisdom, and that understanding that goes beyond anything we could know on our own? God's presence is what keeps us safe, makes us feel secure, keeps us on the right path, and gives us hope. Without it, we are truly hopeless people.

Doesn't that just fit as a description of King Saul? As a king who could follow rules, he rocked. As a king who could follow God, he failed. And that is where David excelled.

Bringing the presence of God into the center of your world is brilliant.

God prefers someone who will listen to him, to someone who will just follow rules. Be David on this one and get the presence of God at the center of your life. Don't be Saul. Consider this: when Saul was following all of the rules to a T and carefully making sure he did not break the commands that were placed on the king in Exodus, he thought he was doing everything God really wanted. What he wasn't doing was using the most significant tool he had been given. The ark of the covenant represented the very presence of God with his people. Why would Saul not go there? The answer is simple. Saul was practicing a religion, and obedience, at least for the most part, was what he gave to God.

David learned to practice a relationship with God, and so what he gave to God was more than just obedience; it was devotion from the heart.

If you ever have to choose, choose relationship over religion every time.

A relationship is so much more than religion. Honestly, religion is one-directional. It asks, "What can I do for my god?" A relationship goes both ways. God is interested in me and desires to know me and bless me and love me. In return, I am interested in him and desire to know him and bless him and love him. When we practice that kind of Christianity, we live in a deep, trusting relationship with God. When I am simply practicing religion, I live in a deep fear and mistrust of God. Maybe I didn't do the sacrifice right? What if I forgot to pray the right prayer on the right day at the right hour? What if I fail? These insecurities are rampant in religious forms that practice only religion and cannot be based on relationship. Christianity—through the relationship established with his people in the Old Testament and the redemption established through Jesus in the New Testament and the powerful presence of the Holy Spirit placed in the hearts of people in Acts—is the only religion that offers the possibility of a direct relationship with God.

Let me say it again.

If you ever have to choose, choose relationship over religion every time.

34

Worshiping in God's Righteousness

When they came to the threshing floor of Nakon, Uzzah reached out and took hold of the ark of God, because the oxen stumbled. The LORD's anger burned against Uzzah because of his irreverent act; therefore God struck him down, and he died there beside the ark of God. Then David was angry because the LORD's wrath had broken out against Uzzah, and to this day that place is called Perez Uzzah. David was afraid of the LORD that day and said, "How can the ark of the LORD ever come to me?" He was not willing to take the ark of the LORD to be with him in the City of David. Instead, he took it to the house of Obed-Edom the Gittite. The ark of the LORD remained in the house of Obed-Edom the Gittite for three months, and the LORD blessed him and his entire household.

—2 Samuel 6:6–11

As the excitement built and the people reveled in the joy of seeing the presence of God move in their midst, something went terribly wrong. Uzzah touched the ark. That just wasn't allowed. The ark, as the very seat of God, was too holy to be touched by anyone. In fact, to do so was to disrespect the very presence of the God of Heaven. It may not seem like much today, but it was the command of God, and that teaches us some lessons.

God's presence must be properly handled.

Now, I just finished telling you to always choose relationship over religion, but the religious rules do matter to God. The worship of God and the presence of God must be handled in a proper manner. To refrain is showing disrespect to the very God we say we are worshiping. Today, there are no items so sacred that they should never be touched. We do have the very presence of God living within us. We cannot flaunt that presence, or somehow use that presence of God to lord over other people. So often people who have powerful spiritual lives are tripped up by the arrogance that can build within a person as the Holy Spirit uses them powerfully. When that happens, we can fall into the trap of believing that somehow this power is ours.

That is not safe.

God's presence must be properly respected.

When folks start to believe that they can command the Holy Spirit, they are in essence reaching out and taking hold of the ark. They are taking their human hands and attempting to use them to steer the Almighty. I find that terrifying. I have often changed channels or even felt the need to leave the room because some individual began to demand action on the part of God. We cannot do that. We must not do that.

It's disrespectful.

"Well, but Brother Mike, if we pray the prayer right and apply the oil right and have our faith right, then God has to answer." Wait, did you say God has to answer? He is God, and he doesn't have to do anything. "Now, Brother Mike, you just calm down. It's not that we are commanding God. We are just following his rules, and he cannot fail to follow his own rules." Really? Like when he said in the Ten Commandments not to lie, and then he blessed Rahab the prostitute by placing her in the lineage of King David and Jesus for—wait for it—lying?

You see, God's ways are not our ways, and God's thoughts are not our thoughts. Even though we think we have him figured out, there is always something he knows and we don't. Therefore, we cannot even begin to assume that we know how to steer or command the hand of God. Honestly, if such a thing were possible, then we would be dealing in witchcraft and not Christianity.

God's presence, properly handled, brings blessings.

So David was afraid of God and the ark. I mean, it had just killed a guy. So he left it at the house of Obed-Edom "and the LORD blessed him and his entire household" (2 Sam. 6:11). When we learn to rightly handle the presence of the Lord in our lives, God's blessings will flow. That doesn't mean that nothing bad will ever happen. It just means that when it does, we are not left on our own.

35

Worshiping in God's Presence

Now King David was told, "The LORD has blessed the household of Obed-Edom and everything he has, because of the ark of God." So David went to bring up the ark of God from the house of Obed-Edom to the City of David with rejoicing. When those who were carrying the ark of the LORD had taken six steps, he sacrificed a bull and a fattened calf. Wearing a linen ephod, David was dancing before the LORD with all his might, while he and all Israel were bringing up the ark of the LORD with shouts and the sound of trumpets. As the ark of the LORD was entering the City of David, Michal daughter of Saul watched from a window. And when she saw King David leaping and dancing before the LORD, she despised him in her heart. They brought the ark of the LORD and set it in its place inside the tent that David had pitched for it, and David sacrificed burnt offerings and fellowship offerings before the LORD. After he had finished sacrificing the burnt offerings and fellowship offerings, he blessed the people in the name of the LORD Almighty. Then he gave a loaf of bread, a cake of dates and a cake of raisins to each person in the whole crowd of Israelites, both men and women. And all the people went to their homes.

—2 Samuel 6:12–19

David heard that the house of Obed-Edom was being blessed by the presence of the ark of the Lord, and he got some advice on how to properly handle the ark. Then he went out to try again. You see, when they went to get the ark the first time, they placed it on a new cart. That wasn't how it was to be moved. The ark was to be moved by special poles through special rings placed on each corner of the ark itself. It was to be carried by the priests. Here is the warning to those priests:

After Aaron and his sons have finished covering the holy furnishings and all the holy articles, and when the camp is ready to move, only then are the Kohathites to come and do the carrying. But they must not touch the holy things or they will die.

—Numbers 4:15

So once David found the proper way to move the ark of the Lord, the party was back on.

Worship, done right, brings you home.

Now they were making progress, but it was slow. Every six steps taken by the priests who were carrying the ark were marked by another sacrifice. This is really fitting. As the presence of God is returning to the center of your life, the process of sacrificing everything you have to him takes time. It sometimes seems like every few steps, we find something else that is getting in the way of our relationship with God. We need to take the time to stop, burn it off, and move on. It can be a long process but it ultimately leads us home. When the spirit of God is fully established at the center of our lives, things really begin to change.

Furthermore, do you see the harkening back to Genesis here? The priests took six steps and offered praise to God on the seventh. Listen to the command of Moses from Exodus 20:11: "For in six days the LORD made the heavens and the earth, the sea, and all that is in them, but he rested on the seventh day. Therefore the LORD blessed the Sabbath day and made it holy." King David was revisiting God's commands with every step toward the ark's final resting place. He was modeling the rhythm of Jewish culture and honoring the God of that culture by the way they walked as they carried the ark of God.

Beautiful.

Worship, done right, brings joy.

So there he was, the new king of Israel dancing and jumping around like a little kid who had just won a year's supply at the candy store. David was so filled with joy at that moment that he just could not contain himself. That is what worship does inside of us when we are properly prepared for it. I have been a worship leader and a singer most of my life. I can tell you without hesitation that when I am prepared musically for a worship set and prepared spiritually for the worship time, the result is powerful. The entire band or choir can get lost in the moment, and the power of the Spirit can just sweep away everyone involved. I truly wish that everyone could experience that. There is just nothing like singing at the top of your lungs to a God who has given his all to have a relationship with you. You know the singing doesn't have to be all that great to bless the heart of God. I don't get the feeling that King David was winning any dancing contests with his efforts here on the streets of Jerusalem. However, there was no doubt that he was filled with the joy that comes from the presence of God. That always brings joy to the heart of God.

Worship, done right, results in blessing.

"After he had finished sacrificing the burnt offerings and fellowship offerings, he blessed the people in the name of the LORD Almighty" (2 Sam. 6:18). There is a reward for those who do the work of sacrificing all that God asks. They become a blessing to all those around them. As King David was bringing in the ark of the Lord to Jerusalem, he meticulously offered every sacrifice. He must have been exhausted. All those offerings. All that dancing. All that work. It must have taken forever to get this short journey done. David's over-the-top display of sacrifice and offering to the God of heaven made it clear to the people how important and central the presence of God was to him and to them. In doing so, he became a blessing to the people.

Worship, done right, adds value to everyone.

"Then he gave a loaf of bread, a cake of dates and a cake of raisins to each person in the whole crowd of Israelites" (2 Sam. 6:19). Worship, done right, should add value to people. Their lives should be fuller and their souls well fed. Here, King David gave a literal example of the provision that would come from the presence of the Lord being central in Jerusalem. He made certain that no one went hungry this night and that everyone understood that God, and to the best of his ability, their king, would provide for them.

Praise the Lord!

36

Worshiping in Spite Of Man's Criticism

When David returned home to bless his household, Michal daughter of Saul came out to meet him and said, "How the king of Israel has distinguished himself today, going around half-naked in full view of the slave girls of his servants as any vulgar fellow would." David said to Michal, "It was before the LORD, who chose me rather than your father or anyone from his house when he appointed me ruler over the LORD's people Israel—I will celebrate before the LORD. I will become even more undignified than this, and I will be humiliated in my own eyes. But by these slave girls you spoke of, I will be held in honor." And Michal daughter of Saul had no children to the day of her death.
—2 Samuel 6:20–23

Michal, one of David's wives, was a bit of a problem for him. We first encounter her while Saul was trying to kill David. Saul learned that Michal and David kind of had a thing for each other, so he made a bet with David. King Saul sent word saying: "The king wants no other price for the bride than a hundred Philistine foreskins, to take revenge on his enemies." Saul's plan was to have David fall by the hands of the Philistines (1 Sam. 18:25). That is a pretty gruesome start to a marriage. Instead of an engagement ring from the local jewelry store, David brought Michal—well, you get the picture. David did not disappoint. In fact, he brought Saul twice the number of foreskins from dead Philistines as requested, and Michal became his wife. Then her father gave her in marriage to Paltiel son of Laish—who seemed to really love her, based on his reaction to her being taken back to David in 2 Samuel 3:13–16. She was returned to David physically, but she did not seem to love him any longer.

It seems that after all of the jerking around by the men in her life, Michal became a little bitter. Who could blame her? She was sold for the genital skin of one hundred dead men, forced out of that marriage and into another so that her father could attempt to embarrass David, fell in love with that guy, only to be forced back to David by her brother, Ish-Bosheth, in an attempt to take the throne from David after the death of their father, Saul. It had been rough. A critical spirit hurts us deeper than we realize.

A critical spirit misses the point.

Picture the scene. Michal was looking out her window at the city of Jerusalem. There was celebration and joy everywhere, with singing, dancing, excitement—a real party atmosphere. Everyone was happy, except for Michal. Looking out the window, she only saw David—dancing, wearing next to nothing, and looking like a fool, to her at least. She despised him.

This is what a critical spirit can do to us. It can cause us to miss the most important things in life. Michal completely missed the point that the presence of God was back at the center of his people. She completely missed the fact that her husband was the one credited with bringing the nation together and bringing the ark, which her father had ignored, back to the center of Jewish life where it belonged. She missed all of that because she was bitter.

A critical spirit misses the party.

While everyone else was attending a party, Michal was upstairs planning an argument. She carefully thought through how she would greet David when he got home. She considered the tone she would use in order to make sure she got her point across. She searched for the most cutting words she could find to inflict as much pain and shame as possible. She planned her attack carefully, while everyone else partied.

A critical spirit misses the joy.

Michal put her plan into action when David got home. She made sure she told him how foolish he had looked, how unroyal he had acted, and how even slave girls knew better than to act like that. "And besides, you can't even dance." Well, I added that one, but I bet she said something of the sort. Everyone else in Jerusalem was exhausted with joy. God had given birth to hope through David and his rule. Now, because of her bitterness, Michal would give birth to nothing.

So it is with us. So many times I have watched as people in a given church miss the joy of revival, the power of a well-delivered sermon, or the awe of worship lost in God's powerful presence—all because they're bitter over some decision from years ago. They are so bitter that they miss all of that.

It's sad really.

I would love to tell you that I have never fallen victim to this myself, but I have.

We absolutely must make certain that bitterness is never allowed to steal our joy. There is nothing so important that it's worth missing the powerful movement of the spirit of God. If that happens in the midst of a room I don't like, music I don't like, a preacher I don't like, or a place I don't like, I pray the Holy Spirit will check my attitude so I don't miss his presence.

37

Worshiping Anywhere and Everywhere

Praise the LORD. Praise God in his sanctuary; praise him in his mighty heavens. Praise him for his acts of power; praise him for his surpassing greatness. Praise him with the sounding of the trumpet, praise him with the harp and lyre, praise him with timbrel and dancing, praise him with the strings and pipe, praise him with the clash of cymbals, praise him with resounding cymbals. Let everything that has breath praise the LORD. Praise the LORD.

—Psalm 150

In the end, this is what it really is all about. Our lives are meant to bring glory to God, our Creator. We should praise the Lord through everything we do and everything we say.

Years ago, I sat down and began to list the awesome titles and reality of who this God is that we serve. I attempted to think of every title and attribute. I began to arrange these in such a way that they had a bit of a flow to them. Then, at the end of a sermon on worship, I read it to the congregation. Since that Sunday in Hickory, North Carolina, I have read that long poem in numerous locations, and it has always had the same effect. People worship freely and are newly amazed at this God they have been serving all along. This little poem has shown up all over the internet; it has been published in books and curriculum I have nothing to do with. It has been credited to me and listed as "author unknown." It ended up on one YouTube video being read by an eleven-year-old in a Lutheran church. It's pretty cool, actually. What gives it power is the fact that it only talks about who God is, and so I want to wrap up our time together with the best "Praise the Lord" thing I have ever written.

After you read it . . .

Remember . . .

This is the God we serve. Praise him!

God is Lord Almighty, Omnipotent King, Lion of Judah, Rock of Ages, Prince of Peace, King of Kings, Lord of Lords, Provider, Protector, Paternal Leader, Ruling Lord, and Reigning King of all the universe. He is Father, he is Helper, he is Guardian, and he is God.

He is the First and Last, the Beginning and the End. He is the keeper of creation and the Creator of all he keeps. The Architect of the universe and the Manager of all times.

He always was, he always is, and he always will be. Unmoved, Unchanged, Undefeated, and never Undone.

He was bruised and bought healing. He was pierced and eased pain. He was persecuted and bought freedom. He was dead and bought life. He is risen and brings power. He reigns and brings peace.

The world can't understand him, the armies can't defeat him, the schools can't explain him, and the leaders can't ignore him. Herod couldn't kill him, the Pharisees couldn't confuse him, the people couldn't hold him. Nero couldn't crush him, Hitler couldn't silence him, the New Age can't replace him, and the atheists can't explain him away.

He is Light, Love, Longevity, and Lord. He is Goodness, Kindness, Gentleness, and God. He is Holy, Righteous, Mighty, Powerful, and Pure. His ways are right, his word is eternal, his will is unchanging, and his mind is on me. He is my redeemer, he is my savior, he is my guide, he is my peace. He is my joy, he is my comfort, he is my Lord, and he rules my life.

I serve him because his bond is love, his burden is light, and his goal for me is abundant life. I follow him because he is the Wisdom of the wise, the Power of the powerful, the Ancient of days, the Ruler of rulers, the Leader of leaders, the Overseer of the overcomers, and the Sovereign Lord of all that was and is and is to come.

If that seems impressive to you, try this for size. His goal is a relationship with ME. He will never leave me, never forsake me, never mislead me, never forget me, never overlook me, and never cancel my appointment in his appointment book.

When I fall, he lifts me up. When I fail, he forgives. When I am weak, he is strong. When I am lost, he is the way. When I am afraid, he is my courage. When I stumble, he steadies me. When I am hurt, he heals me. When I am broken, he mends me. When I am blind, he leads me. When I am hungry, he feeds me. When I face trials, he is with me. When I face persecution, he steels me. When I face problems, he comforts me. When I face loss, he provides for me. When I face death, he carries me home.

He is everything for everybody, everywhere, every time, and every way. He is God, he is faithful, I am his, and he is mine. My Father in heaven can whip the father of this world, and so, if you're wondering why I feel so secure, understand this: He said it, I believe it, and that settles it. God is in control, I am on his side, and that means all is well with my soul.